Gospelizers!

Terrorized
and
Intensified

Rev. Dr. Walter Arthur McCray

"How beautiful are the feet of Gospelizers!"

(Romans 10:15b)

BLACK LIGHT FELLOWSHIP
Chicago, Illinois

Gospelizers! Terrorized and Intensified

Copyright © 2002. Walter Arthur McCray.
All Rights Reserved.
Rev. Dr. Walter Arthur McCray

BLACK LIGHT FELLOWSHIP
P. O. Box 5369 • Chicago, Il 60680
(773) 826-7790 FAX - (773) 826-7792
w w w . g o s p e l i z e r s . c o m

Unless otherwise noted, Bible quotations are from the *New Revised Standard Version Bible* Copyright © 1989, Division of Christian Education of the National Council of the Churches of Christ in the Unites States of America. Used by permission. All rights reserved.

Scripture quotations marked (NLT) are taken from the *Holy Bible, New Living Translation,* copyright 1996. Used by permission of Tyndale House Publishers, Inc., Wheaton, Illinois 60189. All rights reserved.

Cover: Troy Brown Design, *Lafayette, IN*
Copy Editor: Mary C. Lewis, *Chicago, IL*

ISBN: 0-933176-50-3
LOC: 2002007761

Library of Congress Cataloging-in-Publication Data

McCray, Walter Arthur.
  Gospelizers! : terrorized and intensified / Walter Arthur McCray.
      p. cm.
Includes bibliographical references and index.
  ISBN 0-933176-50-3
1. Evangelistic work. 2. Blacks--Religion. I. Title.
  BV3793 .M34 2002
  266--dc21
                                    2002007761

02 03 04 05 06 07 08 09 10 — 10 9 8 7 6 5 4 3 2 1

Printed in the USA.

With much

love, respect, and debt

to

The Reverend Dr. Arthur D. Griffin

My Father in the Gospel Ministry

and a

Gospelizer!

Jesus said,
"The Spirit of the Lord is upon me
because he has anointed me
to *gospelize* the poor."
(Luke 4:18a)

"But [Jesus] said to them,
'I must *gospelize* the kingdom of God to the other
cities also; for I was sent for this purpose.'"
(Luke 4:43)

"And [Jesus] answered them,
'Go and tell John what you have seen and heard:
the blind receive their sight, the lame walk, the lepers
are cleansed, the deaf hear, the dead are raised,
the poor are *gospelized*.'"
(Luke 7:22)

"Soon afterwards
[Jesus] went on through cities and villages,
proclaiming and *gospelizing* the kingdom of God.
The twelve were with him, as well as some women…"
(Luke 8:1-2a)

"Now those who were scattered
went from place to place,
gospelizing the word."
(Acts 8:4)

"Thus I make it my ambition to *gospelize*
not where Christ has already been named…"
(Romans 15:20)

"How beautiful are the feet of
Gospelizers!"
(Romans 10:15b)

(NRSV, with key term literally translated.)

In witness of *Gospelizers!*

"When you first read to the NBCSC committee a page contrasting names of Christ's followers with your new name 'Gospelizers,' I knew right then your work would leave a lasting impact. The finished product magnifies my expectation. **Gospelizers!** exhibits your deep commitment to Christ, and ability to create Biblical Christ-centered literature at its best to God's glory. Its 'Good News' message is rich and deserves careful consideration by students and other Christian leaders."
Ruth Lewis Bentley, Ph.D., Co-Founder,
National Black Christian Students Conference

"I enjoyed reading **Gospelizers!**...and approve enthusiastically. You have exhibited very careful study and have integrated this into your rich experience in church ministries. 'Gospelizing' and 'Koinonia-izing' have given a fresh exhortation to the ministries of the Church in a time of crisis. I am confident that **Gospelizers!** will be very helpful to both pastors and church members as they gain a holistic perspective on the ministries of the Church...I am so impressed with your dynamic experiences in the Spirit..."
Dr. Norman R. Ericson, Professor Emeritus of
New Testament Studies, Wheaton College

"Once again a unique gift and prophetic word has emerged from the fellowship of NBEA. **Gospelizers!** fits the bill. Its emphasis on the holistic salvation, righteousness, and koinonia of the Gospel speaks clear. So does the call for Christ's church to grow by multiplication. I'm glad to support your message, and heartily commend it to all theologically inclined, mission-minded, and forward thinking believers and churches, Black and white alike."
Rev. Clarence L. Hilliard, Board Chairman,
National Black Evangelical Association

"You have hit the nail right on the head! **Gospelizers!** will make some strong waves both inside Black Christian communities and beyond....Thank you for not quenching the Spirit. I am now ready to use your first-choice word 'gospelizing'...**Gospelizers!** affected me as I read it and will effect changes in the way I talk about God's call on my life and His mandate to the Church. **Gospelizers!** is a good thing that emerged from the disaster of 9-11-01."
Jim Wilson, African American Relations,
Wycliffe Bible Translators

In witness of *Gospelizers!*

"**Gospelizers!** *presents a re-emerging paradigm that has a consistent Christ-centered message for humanity. It provides the Biblical basis and challenges the Church to become fully empowered in the holistic redeeming mission of Christ.* **Gospelizers!** *is compelling and deserves to be read and heeded by Christ's Church at large.*"

Atty. Lester L. Barclay, Church Administrator,
Progressive Beulah Pentecostal Church

"*I rejoice in your re-centeredness in Christ and praise God for this awesome work he is doing in your life. Sometime ago, my missionary colleagues and I were discussing the...need for a different word....I believe...***Gospelizers!** *is the answer to our prayers...and is destined to revolutionize the understanding of missions in the Christian community.*"

Rev. Ivor Duberry, Director,
African American Center for World Mission

"*I am proud to affirm* **Gospelizers!** *Dr. Walter McCray, as usual in all of his writings, uncovers the true meanings of words, and their needed importance for making the Gospel message more relevant to all people.*"

Rev. Dr. Benjamin W. Johnson, Sr., President,
Christian Creative Ministries

"*In* **Gospelizers!***, Dr. Walter Arthur McCray has struck a new note on the ageless theme of what it means to witness for Jesus Christ. This priority compels action from every person and every church that claims the Name of the Lord. It is a 'must read.'*"

Dr. Jack Estep, Executive Administrator,
CBAmerica

"*The subject of evangelism and missions is so near and dear to the heart of God. Therefore, it should be near and dear to our hearts. I commend Dr. Walter McCray for reminding us, as the church of Jesus Christ, of this vital subject –* **Gospelizers!** *Our churches are at a dangerous point because many are turning inward instead of turning outward. We all need to rededicate ourselves to the task of gospelizing and disciple-making. Reading* **Gospelizers!** *will help motivate us to greater commitment to the mission and ministry of Jesus Christ.*"

Brian Johnson, National Coordinator, The Cooperative
Missions Network of the African Dispersion (COMINAD)

Gospelizers!
Terrorized
and
Intensified

Rev. Dr. Walter Arthur McCray

Gospelizers are God-sent messengers whose holistic witness brings the Good News of Christ's presence and redeeming mission to humanity.

"Gospelizers"

Formed with *"Gospel,"* meaning *"Good News."*
Derived from Greek *"a proclaimer or bringer of good news,"* or *"to tell or bring good news; to announce or bring the gospel"* [*euangelistes* or *euangelizo;* both from *angelos,* *"messenger, angel,"* and *eu, "good"*].

Gospel + *ize* + *er* + *s* = *Gos · pel · iz · ers*

The Identity and Mission Imperative
of Christ's Messengers

How the word *"Gospelizers"* is formed.

$$\underline{\textit{Gospel}} + \underline{\textit{ize}} \quad + \quad \underline{\textit{er}} \quad + \quad \underline{\textit{s}} \quad = \quad \underline{\textit{Gos} \cdot \textit{pel} \cdot \textit{iz} \cdot \textit{ers}}$$

	Gospel	*(a noun)*
+	*ize*	*(a verb-forming suffix)*
=	*Gospelize*	*(a verb; denoting the activity)*
		(changing the noun into a verb;
		a verbalized noun)
+	*er*	*(a noun-forming suffix)*
+	*s*	*(plural)*
=	*Gospelizers*	*(a noun, pl.)*
		(indicating persons who do the activity)
		(changing the noun that was verbalized
		back to a noun)

Table of Contents

Preface

"The human mind plans the way, but the Lord directs the steps" (Proverbs 16:9). Some things are finished in a manner and for a purpose that differs from their beginning. The present case in point is *Gospelizers!*

This book began as an overall vision/strategic plan for my pastorate. However, it soon became apparent that my thinking was too circumscribed. My desire to keep the message applicable and communicable to my immediate ministry was repressing my freedom and creativity of thought. Attempts to tailor my words exclusively for my church family—which amounted to trying to pour "new wine" into "old wineskins"—were not working. A well-meaning aim to meet a particular need was hindering deeper insights, preventing me from expressing and applying a more pertinent truth.

Not too long into the writing process, I clearly heard the Lord speaking: "You can't just write for the church you are pastoring. The message I am giving you is for *the* Church." In response, and in stages, I switched gears. I began to broaden my outlook and write for Christ's Church at large. Then my freedom came. The fuller message began unfolding, with fresh insights and radical challenges. As these and other changes took place, the vision broadened. I focused my research and writing on producing a manuscript with a word for wider publication. *Gospelizers!* is the end result and the Lord-directed fruit of my steps.

Whether for African Americans or whites, broad-based Church audiences are the intended readers of *Gospelizers!* The book naturally appeals to Christians who appreciate in-depth Bible study, and to all believers who desire to serve Christ by reaching out with salvation and ministry to people everywhere.

Gospelizers! can be used in several ways. At baseline, this work is simply a Biblical word-study *(euangelizo)*. As explained in the Scripture, *euangelizo* heightens the awareness of our identity as witnesses for Christ. For spiritual enrichment, *Gospelizers!* provides a positive outlook for the Christian community in a post-September 11th "terrorized" world. Believers always have "Good News" in Christ. We can also appreciate *Gospelizers!* as an evangelism/missions resource with applications for believers and churches' mission-purpose. The book makes an appeal to the Christian community—especially Black believers and our churches—to become urgently serious about answering God's call to holistic mission, both at home and abroad (see the Bibliography for resources related to Blacks and mission). On these pages, Church growth and development enthusiasts will find significant direction for receiving new converts, and for teaching, training, and empowering believers as Christ's disciples. The Biblical data and principles highlighted in *Gospelizers!* can assist our theologically inclined readers in forming and practicing their missiology—theology of missions (see chapter 8). *Gospelizers!* also is a testimony to God for renewing my life (see chapter 1). I am recentered in Christ, have rearranged my priorities, and thank the Lord for His patience and pushing!

As a paradigm (an example serving as a model) for Christian identity and mission, we trust Christ will use *Gospelizers!* to capture our spiritual imagination and energies. Through these the Lord will quicken each of us His followers to effectively receive the charge of His mission-assignment: **"Peace be with you. As the Father has sent me, so I send you"** (John 20:21b, emphasis mine).

As usual, I owe much gratitude to many persons for their help, encouragement, support, and especially their prayers. I needed them during the manuscript development and this challenging period of my sojourn. First is my loving wife, Thelma, who faithfully stands with me and empathetically shares my dreams and changes.

I thank both Mary C. Lewis for her conscientious and very professional copyediting, and Troy Brown for his usual great creativity and flexibility in cover design. Also, my thanks to each who read the manuscript and offered insights and suggestions.

In closing, let me thank my God by borrowing the words of the Apostle Paul: "I am grateful to Christ Jesus our Lord, who has strengthened me, because he judged me faithful and appointed me to his service..." (1 Timothy 1:12). "But I do not count my life of any value to myself, if only I may finish my course and the ministry that I received from the Lord Jesus, **to testify to the good news of God's grace**" (Acts 20:24, emphasis mine).

Rev. Dr. Walter Arthur McCray
March 31, 2002
33rd Year in the Gospel Ministry

"Gospelizers"
is an identity and mission imperative of Christ's messengers.

"Gospelizers" is a novel word for our needful world.

The name *"Gospelizers"* is formed with
"Gospel," meaning "Good News."
"Gospelizers" is a literal equivalent of the Biblical Greek.
"Gospelizers" is a recovered term being pressed into service
as a select name and paradigm for Christian mission.

"Gospelizers" is the recommended name-of-choice
best identifying messengers of God who bring
the "Good News" of Christ's presence by their holistic
witness on His redeeming mission to all humanity.

Gospelizers bring good words, gracious works,
and great workings of God in their witness.
The movement of growth goes from developing
disciples into *Gospelizers* into churches.
Gospelizers are the bridge between making disciples
for Christ to holistically ministering in the community.
Gospelizers are the connection between holistic ministry in
the community and multiplying churches for Christ.

Without *Gospelizers*, the
Christian community becomes ingrown,
and making disciples becomes socially imbalanced.
Without *Gospelizers*,
"the lost," "the least/poor," and "the unwell" of the
harvest-fields are forsaken by the followers of Christ.
Without *Gospelizers*,
multiplying churches for Christ
becomes accidental or exceptional.

Without *Gospelizers*, worship of God becomes
profane, hypocritical, and socially pacifying.
Gospelizers are the cyclical path from joyful worship to
community ministry and back to joyful worship!

Introduction

One select word captures the essence of believers' witness to the world for Christ in these trouble-laden days: "Gospelizers." Believers are "Gospelizers" with and for Christ. "Gospelizers" is a novel word for our needful world.

Obviously, the heart of *Gospelizers* is *Gospel*. In essence, the term identifies those who spread the Gospel of Christ, Christ's *Good News*.

Gospelizers is not a recently discovered word, nor has this author coined it. The term is being uncovered. A general search shows that Gospelizers albeit used most sparingly, has existed for hundreds of years in one form or another. Mainly, it is defined in word studies and commentaries; or it appears in mission-oriented topics.[1] In the present treatment, Gospelizers is being recovered and reintroduced to the wider Christian community. This excellent word is a paradigm for Christ's followers and our witness for Him. As such, **Gospelizers defines and manifests an identity and mission imperative for messengers of Christ.** The book explains this idea and draws applications for believers and our churches.

Gospelizers! has three parts: "Impetus and Imperative," "Identity and Paradigm," and "Development and Destination." Throughout these sections, *"Gospelizers"* is elucidated in three ways. We understand the idea 1) by the term's definition, 2) by seeing its use in the models of Jesus and of His followers, and 3) by related Scriptural teachings. Viewed together, a full picture emerges that portrays believers spreading a holistic witness for Christ through their words, works, and miraculous workings. Essentially *all* believers have the potential to be Gospelizers.

"Part I: Impetus and Imperative" gives the motivation and urgency of Gospelizers! The personal impact of September 11, 2001 on my life helped to crystallize the idea and give birth to the book. The context of this catalyst is described in a testimony of my life-changing experience. The attacks and repercussions of September 11 also justify the urgency that should be given to gospelizing. The terrorist tragedy and similar "bad news" circumstances besetting humanity make it imperative that all believers as Gospelizers take most seriously and intensify their witness and mission for Christ. We must seize this chaotic season but *kairotic* moment (God's opportune time) of world crises, and hurriedly and effectively bring to humanity the Good News of Christ's presence and redeeming visitation. Toward this end, we call followers of Christ to urgently rearrange priorities and programs, and center them on gospelizing.

We make five specific calls/challenges to believers and churches:

1. **Study carefully the paradigm of "Gospelizers."**

2. **Gospelize with urgency and highest priority.**

3. **Institute a Gospelizers' teaching-discipleship ministry.**

4. **Organize Gospelizers into churches.**

5. **Maximize resources for the Gospelizers' ministry.**

Reprioritizing time by daily meeting and gospelizing demonstrates a church's urgency. The early Church set the pattern for this ministry, and the contemporary Church is encouraged to follow suit. Definitions are given that show the relationship of terrorism-persecution, urgency-imperative, and intensity. In several specific ways believers should move toward becoming intensified witnesses for Christ.

Eternal realities and destinies compel the witness and mission of Gospelizers. A salvation imperative is the overriding urgency that drives their gospelizing. Through sin and separation from God humanity is lost. But whoever calls on the Name of the Lord Jesus shall be saved (see Romans 10:13ff.). To give the lost another chance, it is imperative that Gospelizers gospelize the Gospel of Jesus and the gracious gift of salvation through His Name. The Scripture uplifts gospelizing as the divine duty of believers. This witness is an imperative mission of Christ's disciples.

"Part II: Identity and Paradigm" provides a detailed exposition of Gospelizers, by explaining the term, illustrating its use, and highlighting its models. Amidst terror, Gospelizers became intensified. Among many names that identify followers of Christ, I promote the use of Gospelizers. The "Gospel" in Gospelizers gets at the heart of Christian witness and mission. Gospelizers are "Good News" messengers.

We should come to understand the underlying textual word-family to which Gospelizers belong. The term has a concise translated rendering, a literal equivalent of a Biblical word-family, which is based on two Greek words: "messenger, angel" (*angelos*), and "good" (*eu*). The Greek noun deriving Gospelizers means a proclaimer or bringer of good news (*euangelistes*, translated "evangelist"). The related verb means to tell or bring good news, to announce or bring the Gospel (*euangelizo*). Modern versions offer various translations (e.g., "proclaim," "bring," "announce," (NRSV); "preach," "bring," "show," "declare" (KJV); "preach," "tell," "bring" (NIV) — either specifying or implying "the gospel").

Scripture places abundantly more stress on the activity ("gospelizing," verb) than on the name ("Gospelizers," noun). Thus, the followers of Christ are named/identified by the activity of their mission. Believers are Gospelizers, because in practice and essence we gospelize. The study follows the pattern of Biblical data in this witness and outreach emphasis.

Second, we explain Gospelizers through its use by and about Jesus, and by others, to explain this ministry. Jesus was par excellence of Gospelizers. He is the preeminent paradigm. Also, Gospelizers was naturally applied to Christ's messengers in their social-historical context. Imitating Christ, they too become our paradigms. Models of Gospelizers include "the Twelve" (disciples/apostles), specifically named and many anonymous women, several evangelists, and a wide range of believers in the early Church. Combined with the definition of the word and the paradigms of Christ and His followers, additional Biblical teachings also disclose Gospelizers. Especially helpful are those teachings that enrich our understanding of the Gospel and its ministry.

When taken together, the insights we gain from these three areas reveal the actual drift of Scripture. The gist of the message has *all* believers falling within the purview of Gospelizers. *All* members of the Church are, or ought to become, witnesses for Christ on His redeeming mission to humanity — Gospelizers!

An essential meaning of Gospelizers is expanded, explained and applied in the study. A concise working definition of the concept follows.

Gospelizers are God-sent messengers whose holistic witness brings the Good News of Christ's presence and redeeming mission to humanity.

Throughout the study stress is placed on the holistic witness of Gospelizers. Gospelizing is indeed speaking good words, but more. It is also doing gracious works, and great workings of God (miracles). The gracious works of gospelizing ought to span the entire spectrum of human need, reaching the whole person and all affairs of life. Gospelizing has a collective or communal dimension, as well as a personal element. Gospelizing, Biblically defined, effects holistic redemption.

As indicated by the Scripture, as the Church of Christ,

the earliest believers emerged as urgent, intensified, and effectual Gospelizers in their world. After the fire of Pentecost, persecution ("terrorism") energized them to do the gospelizing that Christ had commanded them all along (cf. Acts 8:1-4ff.). Not dissimilar to the early Church experience, the immediate urgency of Gospelizers in our day stems from our own "terrors." Two cases in point are the attacks of September 11, 2001, which pale in the face of the AIDS/HIV pandemic that is wasting and devastating Blacks in sub-Saharan Africa and throughout North and South America, and is similarly affecting Asians and whites in North America and Europe. Additionally, there are numerous other terrorizing conditions and situations the world over to which Gospelizers ought to respond with holistic gospelizing ministry.

The Biblical exposition of Gospelizers gives direction to theological formation. Essential Scripture data and observations facilitate this process of theological development. A gospelizing theology, or, better, missiology results.

"Development and Destination," Part III, concentrates on the teaching-discipleship ministry of Gospelizers in the Church. This ministry reflects one of the calls/challenges presented to the churches. Further, this ministry is presented in the context of the Church's mission-purpose.

The Church's Mission-Purpose

The **mission-purpose** of the Church is to *gospelize* in the Name of Christ with a view toward organizing other churches — insuring in the process that the trust of the Gospel is committed, preserved, and transmitted personally, ethno-culturally, and globally from one generation of Christ's disciples to the next.

Through an effective teaching-discipleship ministry, Christ's disciples should be transformed into Gospelizers. In turn they should be commissioned to the harvest-fields where they give a holistic witness. Their passion is to bring the "Good News" of Christ and the blessings of His redemption to humanity. With the whole world in its scope, the central focus and thrust of the mission are "the lost," "the least/poor," and "the unwell." In the Name of Christ, the Gospelizers' holistic mission effectually reaches, serves, and empowers people who are marginalized and victimized in our societies, nations, and the world.

As Christ was sent, so Gospelizers are sent to manifest an entire spectrum of "gracious works." What drives their holistic services is the salvation imperative through the Name of Jesus. Conversions to Christ, through holistic witness, are one result. The multiplication of new congregations/churches is another outgrowth of a gospelizing ministry.

Converts must be *"Koinonia-ized"* – i.e., brought into the fellowship and community of the Church. On the one hand, doing gracious works in Gospel-centered ministries is necessary for Gospelizers. However, on the other hand, multiplying churches – as a good work of gathering together believers into Christ's community – is **mandatory**. The first-century church grew by expanding and intensifying its witness, and then multiplying into other churches. Their Church growth was an intentional and spiritually inevitable outcome of gospelizing. Hence, following this model, Gospelizers must multiply into additional churches of Christ in order to receive Christian converts into fellowship, and strengthen, care for, and make them into disciples and Gospelizers.

Effectiveness in gospelizing ministry hinges on (re)structuring our churches for this purpose. Each church should constantly maintain seven basic priorities, and should organize into a "Church-in-Progress" structure and operational groups to facilitate gospelizing and church multiplication. Gospelizers should develop six essential qualities of character. Each church should maximize its human, financial, and other resources for the Gospelizers' ministry. The key is to strategically plan to support ministry and gospelizing ministers, while minimizing resources for unnecessary building programs and capital improvements. The call is to maximize ministry and multiply churches as an alternative to mega-sizing.

The Postscript reminds us that worshiping and giving glory to God is the highest motivation of Gospelizers. Gospelizing both flows from and results in righteous and joyful worship (cf. Acts 13:2ff.; Acts 8:8). Christ commands His messengers to gospelize. Yet, we are also moved by our personal thankfulness to the Lord. He has redeemed us from sin and already blessed us with the grace of His eternal salvation. What greater motivation is there for us to worship God, other than by being living testimonies and showing ourselves grateful witnesses to the gracious Good News of Christ!

Let us worship God and do the work of Gospelizers!

Part I:

Impetus and Imperative

Terrorized to Gospelize.

The September 11, 2001 attack was the immediate impetus that gave birth to *Gospelizers!* Though the message was already in formation, the terror of that tragic Tuesday became its impelling force. Chapter one describes how 9-11 changed my life and ministry, and explains the dynamics that gave birth to *Gospelizers!* The subsequent chapters of this section call the Church to become urgent about our gospelizing.

A five-fold gospelizing challenge is given to Christ's disciples to motivate, guide our personal and collective gospelizing. Christ's followers should intensify their witness, and move their churches toward meeting and gospelizing daily. The goal is to reach out with the Gospel, with a ministry that is holistic. In all our good works, Gospelizers are driven by a salvation imperative. The center of our holistic outreach is the salvation of the lost from their sin and its temporal and eternal consequences, through the redeeming Gospel of Jesus Christ. Gospelizing gives the lost another chance to receive the saving grace of God. The mission of Gospelizers is urgently imperative.

1

Forced to Change — A 9-11 Testimony

> *The Call:*
> * *Gospelize* with urgency and highest priority.

I Watched.

On September 11, 2001 I was driving from my home in Chicago, heading along Madison Street toward the House of Daniel, Outreach Mission Christian Center. The agency provides benevolent holistic services for 50 homeless men on a 24/7 basis. At the time, I was serving the organization as president and CEO. Approaching the mission, I heard a radio broadcast report of a terrorist attack in New York.

When I reached the mission, I parked in the lot and entered the building. A number of the brothers living at the mission were in the fellowship hall, gathered at the TV intently watching reports of the unfolding tragedy.

"Hey, Pastor McCray," one said, "a plane has crashed into the World Trade Center in New York."

As we watched, breathless, we were startled to see a second plane find its target at the trade center's south tower, getting swallowed up in the crash. Right before our eyes, a great center and symbol of global capitalization and world economics was ablaze. Later, the Pentagon was hit. Planes had become bombs. Something very bad was happening. America was under attack. Hundreds of people had already lost their lives; many more were in the process of dying.

Some kind of shock was fast approaching most of us as we observed the frantic news reports. I recall turning from the TV and walking into the office of the mission's program director. He was watching the news through his open door while sitting at his desk. We exchanged greetings, and feebly expressed whatever we could collect ourselves to say at the time about this rapidly developing incident.

I remember saying, "I am glad those planes did not hit those buildings at the bottom. If they had, the whole buildings would probably crash to the ground."

How startled I became a few minutes later.

Once again, in only a few moments, right before our very eyes fixed to the television, we saw the first flaming tower disintegrate in a dense cloud of churning debris and dust! Never had I seen, never in life had I thought, that a sky-scraping structure could fall to pieces from top to bottom. But it did; it fell from high to low, as though it was directly in front of us.

And then, tragically, it happened again to the other tower.

More than witnessing the crumbling towers, in my spirit I saw a dying humanity. Instinctively I knew whoever was in those failing and falling structures was dead. They were lost persons, precious souls. Most likely, many of the victims never knew the Lord and His saving grace. Many of them, perhaps, never made their final peace with God. I was overwhelmed at the sight and disturbed by thoughts of death and eternal-death; I was heart-sick. At that moment the conviction to **urgently** gospelize struck me with force.

I Wept.

I lost it. I broke down and wept. I could not and would not withhold my sorrow. This was not the time to be strong for the others standing around and practice what many believe about male "strength" under pressure — "men don't cry." At that moment, I gave full vent to my innermost feelings and heart-sickness, and expressed my passion for lost souls.

So I did not restrain myself in the midst of my homeless brothers. Many of them did not respond (at least outwardly) as I did. Probably they had learned to cope with life's tragic moments by shielding their emotional pain and resentment. Some of the brothers did not show any deep emotions. Instead, they seemed to watch as they would view a movie — as though the living reality was simply the excitement of a two-hour Hollywood motion picture. But now, not without some interplay of their own insecurities and vulnerabilities, they also watched me their leader. Their pastor was broken without reserve; he weakened and wept deeply in their presence.

I Heard Him.

I wept because I heard and saw the Lord. Perhaps I experienced Him as Job did in his engulfing "storm."[2] As I gazed teary-eyed at the tragic televised scenes, the many current services and activities of my Christian profession passed swiftly through my mind. Within only fifteen to twenty seconds, I reviewed it all, as though I myself were imminently facing death. I saw all the present consumption of my time, energy, and resources. In the storm of the crumbling towers, I heard the Spirit speak to me, in the words of a familiar hymn, capturing an even more familiar spiritual truth:

You may build great cathedrals large or small,
You can build sky-scrapers grand and tall,
You may conquer all the failures of the past,
But only what you do for Christ will last.

Remember only what you do for Christ will last;
Remember only what you do for Christ will last;
Only what you do for Him will be counted at the end,
Only what you do for Christ will last![3]

"Only what you do for Christ will last" was the message the Lord spoke to my heart on that fateful, terrifying September morning. This personal communication evoked some provocative and unsettling questions in my inner and deepest being.

"Didn't I truly know Christ?"
"Wasn't Jesus the foundation of my life?"
"Wasn't I already in the full service of my Lord?"
"Wasn't I serving for God's glory, and not for myself?"
"Didn't my Christian pursuits evince spiritual and eternal values?"
"Wasn't I a faithful and effective witness for the Lord?"
"Was there a deeper spiritual reality and higher call to ministry to which the Lord was moving me?"
"Did my values need rearranging?"

Unexpectedly, these very serious questions raced through my mind. Finding me unprepared, they took me by storm. They were intensely personal, and worked in me a painful self-examination and emptying.[4] In the midst of the "storm" I heard the Lord and saw His glory.

As never before in my life, the Lord questioned me in the September storm of 2001. The Spirit said, "You are doing a whole lot of good things; but what is the '**perfect will of God**' for this time of your life? It's time to change; now." [5]

I Recentered.

Since experiencing the impact of September 11, I have recentered. By God's grace, I am not the same, and hope never again to be the person I was. Several months prior to 9-11, the Lord had already been speaking to me about a redirection of my life and service for Him.[6] However, the Lord's voice intensified on that day, to continue the fulfillment of His will in my life.

Spiritual recentering requires several self-examining questions:

What is the Lord saying to me?

What is His unique claim on my time and life?

What is the personal agenda and destiny to which the Lord has called me?

What is that special once-in-a-lifetime assignment for which the Lord has uniquely suited me?

What calling must I fulfill in the time of God's *kairotic* moment — in His season of imminent opportunity?

In the 9-11 storm, a lesson I had learned on time management and priorities many years ago now presented me with a new challenge. I remembered the lesson, reapplied its truth, and recentered my life in Christ. Let me explain.[7]

I Reprioritized.

Often we put off doing **the most important** things. In their place we substitute what seems to be **urgent** at the moment.[8] We postpone the important, while preoccupying ourselves with doing what is minor. Or we rush to accomplish superficial yet pressing matters. In hindsight, however, many of the daily routines that we think "we've got to do," and "can't put off," often turn out not to have been such a necessity. They were not as crucial as that oft neglected, but most important, God-directed personal agenda.

Sometimes the "good things" that occupy our time subtly eclipse life's **most important things.**[9] Certainly, we are individually gifted to achieve a great variety of good things. And the people whom we help are grateful and show appreciation for our dedicated service. However, spiritual and eternal realities are the most important things. Ultimately they are truly what count. I had to re-learn this lesson.

Over the weeks following September 11, my answer to the Lord's questions was honest and forthcoming. The season had come for me to **reprioritize my values — to elevate the most important things of the Lord for my life, raising them to the status of urgency.** I did not know how much time I had left to fulfill God's will and purpose. Life's circumstances had become sobering, precarious, and "iffy." Consequently, **I began to act urgently on important things;** acting in the "now." I began rearranging my moment-by-moment priorities. I could not and would not continue to do as I always did, for then I would only get what I always got. I was moved to change.

I Changed.

Over the coming months I responded in several ways. I prayed and sought the Lord's face. I confided with my wife and heard her heart, as I pressed my way. I sought spiritual counsel from Brothers and Sisters in the Lord whose wisdom proved most helpful and supportive. Also, I wrote myself a personal strategic plan, carefully recording the Lord's direction. Then I began acting on the instructions I'd received in "the storm."

Taking it step by step, I tendered resignations from management positions I held in several organizations and curtailed my responsibilities. To guard my time, I cut back on certain unnecessary activities. Due to unforeseen circumstances, I attempted one change that yielded a rather painful, but freeing, outcome. Nevertheless, the Lord's will was done.[10] The moves I made adversely affected my financial stability. The lion's share of my professional income sources became disrupted. I found myself (with my wife) once again "living by faith," trusting the good Lord to provide for our needs.[11]

Through these transitions, I embarked upon my life's redirection. I took care of some **important unfinished business.** Once more in my life, I dealt with the most important things in an urgent way and did them in the "now." Changing more rapidly than ever, I felt a renewed call of God. He called me to write the Lord's message, to be accessible and available to spread this message through the Church across the nation, and to experience a time of personal regeneration.[12]

Making these changes in and for the Lord brought a blessing. With a renewed focus of Christ in my life and ministry, I gained an abiding peace. During those days of change, *Isaiah's* word on peace became a refuge for my soul:

> [3] Those of steadfast mind you keep in peace — in peace because they trust in you. [4] Trust in the LORD forever, for in the LORD GOD you have an everlasting rock (Isaiah 26:3-4).

I Re-fired.

The opportunity to **"re-fire the furnace"** of my writing became most important in my redirection. Writing is one of my gifts from God, evident and confirmed by many.[13] I had never doubted the call to write. At times, though, I had sacrificed consistent performance of this gift in order to render good services to others.[14] Now, yet again in my sojourn, I found the time and freedom necessary for writing. I freed myself from certain outside pressures and from unnecessary (and sometimes inhibiting) "good things." In doing so, I redeemed the freedom to spend extended time in studying the Word, in consecration, and in composing my thoughts.

In my renewed call to write, reaffirmed by the September storm of 2001, I was urged and energized by the Lord's words spoken to Habakkuk. Similar terrorizing circumstances troubled the prophet himself.[15] In Habakkuk 2:1-4 we read:

> [1] I will stand at my watchpost, and station myself on the rampart; I will keep watch to see what he will say to me, and what he will answer concerning my complaint. [2] Then the LORD answered me and said: Write the vision; make it plain on tablets, so that a runner may read it. [3] For there is still a vision for the appointed time; it speaks of the end, and does not lie. If it seems to tarry, wait for it; it will surely come, it will not delay. [4] Look at the proud! Their spirit is not right in them, but the righteous will live by their faith.

I Rededicated.

The message at hand, *Gospelizers!*, is the fruit of "re-firing the furnace" of my writing. It is one response to the terrorism of 9-11, and represents an outcome of that important and urgent change of God in my life—working His perfect will.[16] However, the book does not simply show the fruit of my redirection and rededication. I have received the truth of *gospelizing* in my soul and confirmed the renewed impartation of God's change in my life. More than before, I now see myself as a *Gospelizer*. My life has become an urgently renewed journey, and I have a more clearly defined Christian witness and mission.

I deeply sense an urgent conviction to write. Yet, far and beyond my own present calling and work, the ministry of *gospelizing* is and has been God's urgency both for the Church and for these ominous hours and foreboding moments of the world. Of much greater importance and

value than the written product, is the living-epistle manifested in the Christ-centered life and mission experience.

**The good purpose and love of God is that all humanity
becomes effectually impacted by the redemptive
presence of His Son Jesus Christ and the blessings of
grace, truth, and power in the "Good News" brought
to them in person by the *Gospelizers* of His Church.**

Gospelizers! in written form is but one vehicle the Lord
may use to quicken this word in the hearts and lives of His
people. My desire is to help the Lord's people to feel this
calling, see this vision, and embrace its imperatives and
blessings for themselves. Perhaps I can also persuade
some likeminded messengers of the Lord to join with me,
and to travel together by faith on this *Gospelizers'* journey
with and for Christ.

2

A Call for Urgency in the Church

The Call for Intensified Gospelizers

This message is an urgent appeal to believers in Christ and our churches. We have a God-given destiny to fulfill. The appeal is broad-based and straightforward—as followers of Christ we must intentionally become Gospelizers, and intensify our gospelizing. With a more serious and determined focus, we should change our personal ways and church operations to become the Gospelizers Christ meant His disciples to be.

Some Christians are already Gospelizers and some churches are already gospelizing, whether or not they employ those terms. On these pages they will find little or nothing new. We commend these followers of Christ, and encourage them to "keep on keeping on."

However, despite those believers and churches who have grasped with greater clarity and application the continuing witness and mission work of Christ in the world, in the overwhelming majority of the Christian community, there is much room for focus and growth in this area of ministry. Still, whether already "on the case," or "out of the ball park," I believe the information provided in these pages provides creative insights, fresh understanding, and, in some senses, a prophetic outlook. This message is intended to raise the consciousness and intensification of our

Christian witness and mission to a higher level in the Church, especially among believers of African descent.

A Working Definition

Gospelizers **are God-sent messengers whose holistic witness brings the Good News of Christ's presence and redeeming mission to humanity.**

The passion of Gospelizers is to spread Christ's presence with the blessings of His salvation for all the lost, the least/poor, and the unwell in the harvest-fields of the world. Gospelizers bear a holistic witness for Christ by proclaiming good words, performing gracious works, and imparting great/miraculous workings of God. Working with Christ and His Church, the mission of Gospelizers is to urgently and effectually reach out to people who apparently are yet unaffected by the Gospel's grace, truth, and power. Through their holistic witness of Christ's redeeming mission, the aims of Gospelizers are to convert the lost, church the converted, and multiply the churches. Throughout each new generation, Christ has mandated Gospelizers to fulfill their mission by gospelizing to every person, among all nations, to the uttermost parts of the earth, before the end of time, and until the Lord returns.

Based on this definition of Gospelizers, in the Name of the LORD our Christ, we present the following challenges to the disciples of His Church and to their congregations:

> ### The Call to Believers and Churches
>
> 1. Study carefully the paradigm of *"Gospelizers."*
>
> 2. *Gospelize* with urgency and highest priority.
>
> 3. Institute a *Gospelizers'* teaching-discipleship ministry.
>
> 4. Maximize resources for the *Gospelizers'* ministry.
>
> 5. Organize *Gospelizers* into churches.

The goal of this challenge is to motivate and assist Christ's disciples in intentionally becoming intensified Gospelizers, both personally and collectively.

The Call Explained

1. Study carefully the paradigm of "Gospelizers."

Give serious attention to an in-depth study of Gospelizers in Biblical usage, with a view toward adopting this term as an identifying name of Christ's mission-minded messengers. This concept should receive careful Scriptural examination and reflection in both personal devotions and Church instruction classes. Along with study, believers should offer prayers for wisdom, understanding, and obedience to God. In addition, believers should "talk-up" this mission among the saints, and act on this word of Christ.

2. Gospelize with urgency and highest priority.

Believers should deem the present climate of terrorism as a "rise up and reach out" message from God, motivating followers of Christ to fulfill this great responsibility of gospelizing the lost. As courageous warriors of Christ, we must prevent the spirit and acts of terror and terrorizing situations from defeating us—sapping our energy and strength, and diverting our attention and resources away from gospelizing in the world. We must rekindle our passion for God's blessed but dying humanity. We must especially *gospelize* **the victimized and marginalized** – the poor, the afflicted, and the powerless of humanity.

As Christians, it is imperative for us as Christ's messengers to reorder our personal and church priorities, and show it by advancing outreach movements of gospelizing in the Lord's harvest. This is the Church's unique mission, and therefore should be our highest priority. Each congregation must review its agenda for ministry. Where necessary, the Church should refocus and restructure its practices and programs to effectively spread Christ's Good News. Equipped with strategies for taking immediate action, and going forth from our congregations into our communities each church must reach out and gospelize.

3. *Institute a Gospelizers' teaching-discipleship ministry.*

Taking serious action on Jesus' example, teachings, and pattern of training for gospelizing the world, each church should begin an "all leaders required" teaching-discipleship ministry. The three goals of this ministry should be to:

a) Transform disciples into *Gospelizers;*
b) Commission *Gospelizers* to the harvest-fields; and
c) Multiply *Gospelizers* into churches.

This teaching-discipleship ministry should become the normal and recurring practice of an overall church program. Church growth through conversion to Christ will be multiplied both at home and throughout the world, thereby fulfilling Christ's mission.

4. *Organize Gospelizers into churches.*

Churches should organize Gospelizers into churches. This ministry should neither be accidental nor exceptional. Organizing other churches is an act of gospelizing, and a response to the fruit of holistic outreach and growth of church membership. This strategy is also a viable alternative, helping our churches resist an often debilitating and sidetracking "a bigger building is better" mentality.

5. Maximize resources for the Gospelizers' ministry.

This call challenges each church to:

a) Rework our schedules and programs around daily and seasonal gospelizing.

b) Allocate funds and receive special offerings for supporting Gospelizers and their ministry, programs, and activities. Shift certain monies from unnecessary building and capital improvement campaigns to the gospelizing ministry.

c) Make full use of the total space in all existing facilities, including the most often underused worship sanctuary.

Adhering to these practices will keep our churches free to do outreach and attain church growth.

The Urgency of Daily Meeting and *Gospelizing*

How we use our money and time are telling indicators of our values. A glance at our checkbook or cash receipts will quickly reveal our highest priorities. A review of our calendar and how we spend our time is even more revealing. Time is more valuable than money and wealth, and how we use it is more crucial and indicative of our spiritual state than some other signs. Unlike money, all of us have an equal and limited share of time—a precious 24 hours for each day for each of us.

It is imperative that Christ's followers reprioritize time. We cannot package, store, and retrieve time for use in a different set of circumstances. Once time is gone—usefully spent or wasted—it is gone for good. As believers and churches, how we use time is essentially pertinent to the urgency of *Gospelizers* and their ministry. The Word says,

⁵ Conduct yourselves wisely toward outsiders, **making the most of the time.** ⁶ Let your speech always be gracious, seasoned with salt, so that you may know how you ought to answer everyone (Colossians 4:5-6, emphasis mine).

Further,

¹⁵ Be careful then how you live, not as unwise people but as wise, ¹⁶ **making the most of the time,** because the days are evil (Ephesians 5:15-16, emphasis mine).

How we use our time for gospelizing "the kingdom of God and His righteousness" is urgently serious (cf. Matthew 6:33). The time we give each day for this purpose will clearly show our level of commitment to Christ and to His gospelizing and redeeming mission in the world. In this context we need to grasp the import of "one day at a time." The early Church set this pattern. They steadfastly and daily gave themselves to the work of the Lord.

On this topic, the contemporary Church owes a special gratitude to Dr. Arthur D. Griffin, Pastor, Chicago's First Baptist Congregational Church; and President, Chicago Baptist Institute.[17] In word and practice, in preaching and teaching, Dr. Griffin has provided simple Scriptural insights and prophetic and untiring efforts in lifting up the Church's **"daily"** dimension. He exhorts our churches (the local collective people of God) to meet together each and every day of the week — for teaching and prayer, worship and fellowship, and outreach and ministry — in the expectation that the Lord will daily add to the Church those who are being saved (cf. Acts 2:47). Such a daily pattern obviously flows from the gospelizing urgency, and is evidence of the priority time-commitment made by the Church.

Here is the Biblical basis for the Church meeting and gospelizing daily, as modeled by Dr. Griffin.[18]

Jesus taught/gospelized daily

Matthew 26:55

At that hour Jesus said to the crowds, "Have you come out with swords and clubs to arrest me as though I were a bandit? **Day after day** I sat in the temple teaching, and you did not arrest me" (emphasis mine).

Luke 19:47

Every day he was teaching in the temple. The chief priests, the scribes, and the leaders of the people kept looking for a way to kill him (emphasis mine).

Luke 20:1

One day as he was teaching the people in the temple and telling the good news *[gospelizing]*, the chief priests and the scribes came with the elders (emphasis mine).

Luke 21:37

Every day he was teaching in the temple, and at night he would go out and spend the night on the Mount of Olives, as it was called (emphasis mine).

Luke 22:53

"When I was with you **day after day** in the temple, you did not lay hands on me. But this is your hour, and the power of darkness!" (emphasis mine)

The early Church met daily, and the Lord saved daily

Acts 2:46-47

[46] **Day by day**, as they spent much time together in the temple, they broke bread at home and ate their food with glad and generous hearts, [47] praising God and having the goodwill of all the people. And **day by day** the Lord added to their number those who were being saved (emphasis mine).

Acts 5:42

And **every day** in the temple and at home they did not cease to teach and proclaim *[gospelize]* Jesus as the Messiah (emphasis mine).

Acts 16:4-5

4 As they [Paul and others] went from town to town, they delivered to them for observance the decisions that had been reached by the apostles and elders who were in Jerusalem. 5 So the churches were strengthened in the faith and increased in numbers **daily** (emphasis mine).

Acts 17:11-12

11 These Jews [of Berea] were more receptive than those in Thessalonica, for they welcomed the message very eagerly and examined the scriptures **every day** to see whether these things were so. 12 Many of them therefore believed, including not a few Greek women and men of high standing (emphasis mine).

Believers served and encouraged one another daily

Acts 6:1

Now during those days, when the disciples were increasing in number, the Hellenists complained against the Hebrews because their widows were being neglected in the **daily** distribution of food (emphasis mine).

James 2:14-16

14 What good is it, my brothers and sisters,...If a brother or sister is naked and lacks **daily** food, 16...and yet you do not supply their bodily needs...? (emphasis mine)

Hebrews 3:13

But exhort one another **every day**, as long as it is called "today," so that none of you may be hardened by the deceitfulness of sin (emphasis mine).

2 Corinthians 11:28

And, besides other things, I am under **daily** pressure because of my anxiety for all the churches (emphasis mine).

Believers gospelized daily

Acts 5:42

And **every day** in the temple and at home they did not cease to teach and proclaim *[gospelize]* Jesus as the Messiah (emphasis mine).

Acts 17:16-17

16 While Paul was waiting for them in Athens, he was deeply distressed to see that the city was full of idols. 17 So he argued in the synagogue with the Jews and the devout persons, and also in the marketplace **every day** with those who happened to be there (emphasis mine).

Acts 19:9

When some stubbornly refused to believe and spoke evil of the Way before the congregation, he [Paul] left them, taking the disciples with him, and argued **daily** in the lecture hall of Tyrannus (emphasis mine).

The Christ-centered life is a daily experience

Matthew 6:11

Give us this day our **daily** bread (emphasis mine).

Luke 9:23

Then he said to them all, "If any want to become my followers, let them deny themselves and take up their cross **daily** and follow me" (emphasis mine).

1 Corinthians 15:31

I die **every day**! That is as certain, brothers and sisters, as my boasting of you — a boast that I make in Christ Jesus our Lord (emphasis mine).

The Lord is with His Church every day

Matthew 28:20b
"And remember, I am with you always [literally, "all the days"], to the end of the age."

The priority of time given on a daily basis to the *gospelizing* ministry will determine whether our churches become urgent about their witness and mission for Christ Jesus.

The Church's Mission-Purpose

The **mission-purpose** of the Church is to gospelize in the Name of Christ with a view toward organizing other churches — insuring in the process that the trust of the Gospel is committed, preserved, and transmitted personally, ethno-culturally, and globally from one generation of Christ's disciples to the next.

Connecting Ideas

Terrorism-Persecution

The idea of Gospelizers is expressed through the windows of "terrorized" and "intensified." The September 11, 2001 attacks concretely defined terrorism to millions of Americans whose prior ideas were abstract. We now understand terrorism by personal experience and national consciousness.

Terror is intense and sharp; an overmastering of fear with anxiety; it is somewhat prolonged and plays on imagined or future dangers. Terror is frightful violence, bloodshed, and destruction. Terrorists are a group with a political ideology to achieve or maintain their supremacy. Their goal is to create and perpetuate a state of fear and submission. Terrorism may take the form of intimidating threats of violence or coercion, and its targets can be private citizens, public property, or political enemies. It is usually characterized by widespread acts of violence. Terrorism is "terrific," in that it causes great fear and dread. It is very bad and unpleasant; frightful. To terrify is to fill someone with terror and alarm, making them extremely afraid. To become terrorized is to become filled, dominated, or coerced by terror and intimidation. It is to become terror-stricken, terror-struck, terrified.

The Biblical record of **persecution** experienced by the early believers of the Church is related to the idea and experience of contemporary terrorism. To persecute is to oppress or harass an individual or a group with ill-treatment. The pursuit and oppression are persistent. Thus, persecution is a program or campaign to disrupt normal affairs, and drive away, subjugate, or exterminate a people or specific individuals, especially because of their race, ethnic origin, religion, or beliefs. These definitions make clear the connecting lines between contemporary terrorism and Biblical persecution.

Urgency-Imperative

Urgency defines the desired response of Christ's followers to the modern-day terrorism. That which is urgent compels immediate action or attention; it is pressing in importance; imperative. Urgency refers to a degree of importance or its order of priority. Urgent things require or demand immediate attention. An **imperative** need or demand is stronger than urgency. An imperative cannot be deferred or evaded, and usually, it is not possible to revoke. An imperative is a command or plea; a mandatory obligation. Absolutely necessary or required, an imperative cannot be avoided. Inescapable, indispensable, essential, compelling, and exigent are its allies.

Intensity

To be **intense** is to be extreme, have great strength, to show strain, or to deeply feel. Intensity is exceptionally great energy, concentration, strength, power, or force. To be intensive is to be concentrated and exhaustive. An intense person is high, extreme, or very great in some degree, quality or action. Intense persons are strenuous or earnest in their activity, exertion, diligence, or thought.

Toward Becoming Intensified Gospelizers

Gospelizers ought to respond to terrorism by intensifying their witness. We should fight against individualism, social irresponsibility, and personal insensitivity. The personal psycho-social effects of terrorism can be devastating. They can numb a person into withdrawal and engender a dehumanizing spirit. Jesus said, "...because of the increase of lawlessness, the love of many will grow cold" (Matthew 24:12).

Several examples and illustrations will reveal, and help to define and develop strategic approaches to channel gospelizing intensity. Essential approaches have already been given here, in the five-fold call to believers and churches, and in the urgency for the Church to meet and gospelize daily. The lines of thought given below, and explained in subsequent chapters, inform and guide Christ's disciples who desire to become more effective Gospelizers.

Gospelizers should:

- Using the strength and courage of Jesus, overcome the debilitating fears and cowardice associated with being terrorized;

- Recenter in Christ and His will, personally and collectively;
- Respond "now;" with passion and urgency give immediate attention to outreach; but avoid becoming tyrannized by the urgency; be led by the LORD.
- Meet and minister daily;
- Renew viable and effective programs, and redouble efforts; establish new Gospel-centered ministries for outreach;
- Proclaim Christ as the center of gospelizing;
- Do holistic, comprehensive and thorough gospelizing; effect miracles through prayer and impartation;
- Evangelize the lost as the center of holistic gospelizing;
- Multiply churches—by organizing the *Koinonia*, the community and fellowship of Christ's Body—as the center of gracious works in the harvest-fields;
- Clarify the ministry by gaining a good understanding and focus of Gospelizers and gospelizing;
- Prioritize by redressing personal and church priorities in order to concentrate and become more effective in ministry;
- Simplify our lifestyle to keep efforts focused;
- Train and include the whole Church in the whole ministry of gospelizing—men and women, young and old;
- Diversify the church leadership structure;
- Decentralize by promoting outreach and operating from more than a single place;
- Maximize all existing resources and space for gospelizing.

3

Gospelizers' Salvation Imperative

The Call:
- *Gospelize* with urgency and highest priority.

Gospel and Salvation

Gospel and salvation go together. Consider the following truths:

For I am not ashamed of the *gospel; it is the power of God for salvation* to everyone who has faith, to the Jew first and also to the Greek (Romans 1:16, emphasis mine).

In him you also, when you had heard the word of truth, *the gospel of your salvation,* and had believed in him, were marked with the seal of the promised Holy Spirit (Ephesians 1:13, emphasis mine).

Only, live your life in a manner worthy of *the gospel of Christ,* so that, whether I come and see you or am absent and hear about you, I will know that you are standing firm in one spirit, striving side by side with one mind for *the faith of the gospel,* and are in no way intimidated by your opponents. For them this is evidence of their destruction, but of your *salvation.* And this is God's doing (Philippians 1:27-28, emphasis mine).

A definitive teaching of the Scriptures is that all humanity without Christ is lost, destined for eternal damnation apart from the grace of God. The Gospelizers' imperative tells us in no uncertain terms that anyone without Christ is lost, and that salvation from sin and unto God only comes through Jesus' name. "There is salvation in no one else, for there is no other name under heaven given among mortals by which we must be saved" (Acts 4:12). The opposite of salvation is God's judgment upon sin. And that judgment will be according to the Gospel:

> 5 But they will have to give an accounting to him who stands ready to judge the living and the dead. 6 For this is the reason the gospel was proclaimed even to the dead *[even the dead were gospelized]*, so that, though they had been judged in the flesh as everyone is judged, they might live in the spirit as God does (1 Peter 4:5-6).

There is an eternal perdition reserved for all who in this life fail to repent from sin, who fail to place their trust in Christ and His atoning death so they can gain God's free and full forgiveness and righteous pardon. Gospelizers are motivated with urgency to reach our lost world with Christ's redemption. Salvation for the lost from sin and its powers—through the grace, truth, and power of God manifested in Jesus Christ—is the compelling force that keeps driving the holistic nature of Gospelizers' mission.

Why do Gospelizers give witness? They do so to testify of Christ's salvation for sinners. For what purpose are Gospelizers on a mission?[19] As coworkers with our Savior, we go forth to seek and to save the lost. "For the Son of Man came to seek out and to save the lost" (Luke 19:10). Why is there such an important urgency for Gospelizers to reach out to all humanity? Because the Gospel message is "the power of God unto salvation." Multitudes of unrepentant and Gospel-less sinners are living without hope and dying in disbelief day after day.[20] Their experience has been unaffected by the truth, grace and power of the glorious Gospel of Jesus Christ.[21] Let us be warned, the prospect of an eternal future without Christ is hellishly and diabolically horrifying—much more horrifying than any evil destruction of life, such as occurred on September 11, 2001.

> [3] *how can we escape if we neglect so great a salvation?* It was declared at first through the Lord, and it was attested to us by those who heard him, [4] while God added his testimony by signs and wonders and various miracles, and by gifts of the Holy Spirit, distributed according to his will (Hebrews 2:3-4, emphasis mine).

Gospelizing Gives the Lost Another Chance

The Word teaches us that somehow, in some way Christ, as *Gospelizer*, has revealed Himself as a witness to each and every person. John testified: "The true light [Jesus Christ], which enlightens everyone, was coming into the world" (John 1:9). Mark teaches us that the **beginning of the Gospel** was marked by Jesus Christ's appearance on earth: "The beginning of the good news of Jesus Christ, the Son of God" (Mark 1:1). Paul testified, "For the grace of God [Jesus Christ] has appeared, bringing salvation to all" (Titus 2:11).

However, the overwhelming majority of the world's population has not accepted this very mysterious and personal Gospel witness of Jesus Christ Himself. Despite the witness of Christ, several billion people have rejected

Him.[22] They continue in disbelief, not having received the eternal blessings of Christ and His salvation.[23] And there will come "...the day when, according to my [Paul's] gospel, God, through Jesus Christ, will judge the secret thoughts of all" (Romans 2:16).[24]

Herein lies the challenging essence of the Gospelizers' imperative. The continuing witness and mission of gospelizing God gives sinners additional chances to receive Christ and His Gospel of salvation. The power of the Gospel word becomes effectual in the redemption of sinners — even ignorant, blaspheming, and persecuting sinners. Such was Saul of Tarsus (the Apostle Paul) before his conversion to Christ. His redemption was effected by God's mercy and grace.

Paul testified: "...I was formerly a blasphemer, a persecutor, and a man of violence. But **I received mercy** because I had acted ignorantly in unbelief, and **the grace of our Lord overflowed for me** with the faith and love that are in Christ Jesus. The saying is sure and worthy of full acceptance, that Christ Jesus came into the world to save sinners—of whom I am the foremost. But for that very reason **I received mercy,** so that in me, as the foremost, Jesus Christ might display the utmost patience, making me an example to those who would come to believe in him for eternal life" (1 Timothy 1:13-16, emphasis mine).

The grace of the Gospel changed Paul's life. In His first letter to the Corinthians, Paul wrote:

[8] Last of all, as to one untimely born, he [Jesus] appeared also to me. [9] For I am the least of the apostles, unfit to be called an apostle, because I persecuted the church of God. [10] **But by the grace of God** I am what I am, and **his grace toward me** has not been in vain. On the contrary, I worked harder than any of them— though it was not I, **but the grace of God that is with me.** [11] Whether then it was I or they, so we proclaim

and so you have come to believe (1 Corinthians 15:8-11, emphasis mine).

Lest we underestimate the importance of gospelizing the Gospel of God's grace, we have the sharp words Paul wrote to the church of Galatia:

> [6] I am astonished that you are so quickly deserting the one who called you **in the grace of Christ** and are turning to a different gospel—[7] not that there is another gospel, but there are some who are confusing you and want to pervert the gospel of Christ. [8] But even if we or an angel from heaven should proclaim to you a gospel *[gospelize]* contrary to what we proclaimed *[gospelized]* to you, let that one be accursed! [9] As we have said before, so now I repeat, if anyone proclaims *[gospelizes]* to you a gospel contrary to what you received, let that one be accursed! (Galatians 1:6-9, emphasis mine)

Through grace, the Gospel is God's power to save humanity's lost sinners, even to save them "from the guttermost to the uttermost."[25] As Gospelizers we have for our divine use and righteous exploitation our Gospel message! God "decided, through the foolishness of our proclamation *[kerygma]*, to save those who believe" (1 Corinthians 1:21b).

It is imperative for Gospelizers to **rekindle our passion** for God's blessed but dying humanity. It is imperative that we reorder our priorities and **make gospelizing our highest concern.** It is imperative that we **urgently** gospelize **our world as never before.** Millions of persons have yet to be reached with the Gospel.[26] Gospelizers must target them with intensity, wisely using a variety of approaches,[27] and doing our work "at the earliest possible time."[28] The Apostle Paul left us a paradigm:

¹⁸ ...by word and deed, ¹⁹ by the power of signs and wonders, by the power of the Spirit of God...I have fully proclaimed the good news of Christ. ²⁰ Thus I make it my ambition to proclaim the good news *[to gospelize]*, not where Christ has already been named, so that I do not build on someone else's foundation, ²¹ but as it is written, "Those who have never been told of him shall see, and those who have never heard of him shall understand" (Romans 15:18b-21, emphasis mine).

Paul reminded the Church at Corinth, "...we were the first to come all the way to you with the good news of Christ" (2 Corinthians 10:14b).

As we proclaim the Gospel in the power of God, the Word will produce the desired results in the lives of those who hear. It will effect in them "the obedience of faith." As Paul wrote to the church at Rome:

²⁵ Now to God who is able **to strengthen you according to my gospel and the proclamation *[kerygma]* of Jesus Christ,** according to the revelation of the mystery that was kept secret for long ages ²⁶ but is now disclosed, and through the prophetic writings is made known to all the Gentiles, according to the command of the eternal God, **to bring about the obedience of faith** — ²⁷ to the only wise God, through Jesus Christ, to whom be the glory forever! Amen (Romans 16:25-27, emphasis mine).

The Mission Imperative

The following passages illuminate the imperative of the *gospelizing* mission.

Gospelizing was an imperative for Jesus

"The Spirit of the Lord is upon me, because he has anointed me to bring good news to *[gospelize]* the poor."

"But he said to them, 'I must proclaim the good news of *[gospelize]* the kingdom of God to the other cities also; for I was sent for this purpose'" (Luke 4:18, 43; cf. Acts 10:36, Ephesians 2:17).

God calls us to Gospelize

"When he [Paul] had seen the vision, we immediately tried to cross over to Macedonia, being convinced that God had called us to proclaim the good news *[to gospelize]* to them" (Acts 16:10).

Gospelizing is a worthy ambition

"Thus I make it my ambition to proclaim the good news *[to gospelize]* not where Christ has already been named..." (Romans 15:20).

Gospelizing is more substantive than baptizing

"For Christ did not send me to baptize but to proclaim the gospel *[to gospelize]*, and not with eloquent wisdom, so that the cross of Christ might not be emptied of its power" (1 Corinthians 1:17).

There is no substitute for gospelizing the unique, authentic Gospel of Christ

"But even if we or an angel from heaven should proclaim to you a gospel *[gospelize]* contrary to what we proclaimed *[gospelized]* to you, let that one be accursed! As we have said before, so now I repeat, if anyone proclaims to you a gospel *[gospelizes]* contrary to what you received, let that one be accursed!" (Galatians 1:8-9)

*Either we fulfill the mission to gospelize or we suffer the
consequences of failure to discharge this divine duty*

"If I proclaim the gospel *[gospelize]*, this gives me no
ground for boasting, for an obligation is laid on me, and
woe to me if I do not proclaim the gospel! *[gospelize!]*"
(1 Corinthians 9:16)

*Gospelizing the eternal Gospel is effectual for
all the diverse groups of humanity*

"Then I saw another angel flying in midheaven, with an
eternal gospel to proclaim *[to gospelize]* to those who live
on the earth—to every nation and tribe and language and
people" (Revelation 14:6).

Part II:

Identity and Paradigm

> **Emerging Intensified.**

A Recovered Paradigm

There are times when a new paradigm becomes necessary. Due to the critical circumstances of our times, and the mission of Christ's Church, the people of God are in one of those seasons and need a renewed paradigm for the name/identification of believers and our witness.

Alongside other names for Christ's followers, Gospelizers best identifies the messengers of Christ who bring a holistic witness of Christ's presence and redeeming mission to all humanity.[29] The following chapters explain Gospelizers, promote the name, exposit their identity, mission, and witness, highlight Jesus and other Biblical characters who model its meaning, and provide several applications for believers and churches. The closing chapters in this section illustrate how the earliest Gospelizers emerged with intensity amidst the terrorism of their world, and provide insights into developing a theology of gospelizing/Gospelizers.

4

Gospelizer: Definition and Name

> *The Call:*
> • **Study carefully the paradigm of Gospelizers.**

Here we repeat a concise definition of Gospelizers and its elaboration.

> **A Working Definition**
>
> *Gospelizers* **are God-sent messengers whose holistic witness brings the Good News of Christ's presence and redeeming mission to humanity.**
>
> The passion of Gospelizers is to spread Christ's presence with the blessings of His salvation for all the lost, the least/poor, and the unwell in the harvest-fields of the world. Gospelizers bear a holistic witness for Christ by proclaiming good words, performing gracious works, and imparting great/miraculous workings of God. Working with Christ and His Church, the mission of *Gospelizers* is to urgently and effectually reach out to people who apparently are yet unaffected by the

Gospel's grace, truth, and power. Through their holistic witness of Christ's redeeming mission, the aims of Gospelizers are to convert the lost, church the converted, and multiply the churches. Throughout each new generation, Christ has mandated Gospelizers to fulfill their mission by gospelizing to every person, among all nations, to the uttermost parts of the earth, before the end of time, and until the Lord returns.

Gospelizers—The Name

Gospelizers should become well known in Christian vocabulary as a descriptive name for followers of Christ who bear witness on a mission. The paradigm being recommended is not a discovery; it is an uncovering. By recovering the name and the nature of its concept from a measure of obscurity, I hope to promote its use among believers and in the Church.

I am seeking to popularize "Gospelizer." Christians have used the word and similar terms sparingly through the centuries and years.[30] Though its use seems to be rising, I am presently unaware of attempts to press the term into widespread service. However, I would not necessarily be surprised if such were the case. One author notes the evident effectiveness of using gospelize to translate *euangelizo*. Yet, in my estimation he too quickly sets aside its use.[31] There are several potent reasons for encouraging popularity of usage.

Gospelizers is a literal equivalent of its underlying Greek word. It has clarity, force, and immediate significance in the English language. And Gospelizers is a mission-oriented name. Further amplifications and implications of using the word are given below.

A Literal and Great Name to Use

Simply, a "Gospelizer" is "a bringer of good news," and to "gospelize" is to "bring the gospel" (from *euangelizo*). If this definition of *euangelizo* evokes images of an *evangelist* and his/her ministry, then our thoughts are headed in the right direction. "Evangelist" is directly related in meaning to a Gospelizer, just as the underlying terms are directly related. The word translated "evangelist," *euangelistes*,[32] is closely related to *euangelizo*, each being formed from the same root word. True to this meaning, the "evangelists" of the New Testament are the closest identifiably named *"Gospelizers"* in the Church.[33]

"Evangelist" *(euangelistes)* appears only three times in Scripture. In Ephesians 4:11, gifted leaders in the Church are called "evangelists" (used alongside apostles, prophets, pastors and teachers). In Acts 21:8 the Word identifies "Philip the evangelist," who was one of the seven (cf. Acts 6:5). And in 2 Timothy 4:5 Paul instructed Timothy to "do the work of an evangelist."

Though the English term Gospelizers does not appear in Bible translations, it would do a great service for the Church if translations substituted Gospelizers for "evangelist." The term *"Gospelizer"* is a more literal rendering, and carries a more immediate and powerful significance (as noted below). More often than not, we imagine that an evangelist solely preaches or gives verbal witness to win the lost to Christ. Usually, we do not think that the evangelist's good news *works* reach "the least/poor," or perceive the evangelist's *resulting powerful effects* in his/her ministry to the "unwell."[34]

In contrast, the name Gospelizers immediately suggests several very important truths of the Christian faith. Using the term brings to light the revealed truth and content of the Christian message, the Gospel; the personhood and work of Jesus Who is the Subject of the Gospel; the positive character of our message, the "Good News" brought to humanity, as it were, by an angel; the holistic witness in the proclamation, performance, and impartation inherent in the word (as presently defined); and the outreach mission of Christ's messengers.

A Name of Clarity, Force, and Immediate Significance

The "Gospel" in Gospelizers makes the name speak with clarity and force in describing the Christian witness and mission. It conveys immediate significance.

Gospel is Revealed Truth

Using the name Gospelizers keeps the Church focused on the **essential and central revealed truth and content** of our message — the Gospel of Jesus Christ. *"Gospel"* is the root of *Gospelizers*. The Gospel concerns the teachings of Jesus. The Gospel is Christian revelation, the body of divine truth on which the Church stands. The Apostle Paul declared,

> For I want you to know, brothers and sisters, that the gospel that was proclaimed *[gospel that was gospelized]* by me is not of human origin; for I did not receive it from a human source, nor was I taught it, but I received it through a revelation of Jesus Christ (Galatians 1:11-12).

The Gospel of our Lord is the message of the Church. The Good News of Jesus is the very substance of our message. The Lord God has called the Church to "gospelize the Gospel"[35] of Jesus Christ. The Church spreads Gospel, nothing more and nothing less.[36]

> [1] Paul, a servant of Jesus Christ, called to be an apostle, **set apart for the gospel of God,** [2] which he promised beforehand through his prophets **in the holy scriptures,**

[3] the gospel concerning his Son, who was descended from David according to the flesh [4] and was declared to be Son of God with power according to the Spirit of holiness by resurrection from the dead, Jesus Christ our Lord (Romans 1:1-4, emphasis mine).

Jesus Christ is Subject of the Gospel

The name Gospelizers draws us to **Jesus**. Jesus is the Subject of the Gospel. *Matthew, Mark, Luke, and John*, the four Gospels of the New Testament Scriptures, focus and center on Jesus. In their own way, each *Gospel* highlights the Good News brought by the coming of Jesus and His manifestation in the world.[37] Their presentations of Christ during His earthly sojourn[38] concentrate especially on the final three years of Jesus' life and, moreover, on the closing week of His life when Jesus fulfilled the mission work of His Passion—His atoning suffering-death, His burial, His resurrection, and His appearances.

Jesus Christ—the Son and the Messiah of God—is the foundation of Christian faith. And the Gospel that He is in Himself became the preeminent tradition of the Christian Church. As the Apostle Paul wrote:

[1] Now I would remind you, brothers and sisters, of the good news that I proclaimed [*gospelized*] to you, which you in turn received, in which also you stand, [2] through which also you are being saved, if you hold firmly to the message that I proclaimed [*gospelized*] to you—unless you have come to believe in vain. [3] For I handed on to you as of first importance what I in turn had received: that Christ died for our sins in accordance with the scriptures, [4] and that he was buried, and that he was raised on the third day in accordance with the scriptures, [5] and that he appeared (1 Corinthians 15:1-5a).[39]

Also,

> Remember Jesus Christ, raised from the dead, a descendant of David — that is my gospel (2 Timothy 2:8).

Also,

> Others said, "He [Paul] seems to be a proclaimer [*gospelizer*] of foreign divinities." (This was because he [Paul] was telling the good news about Jesus and the resurrection) (Acts 17:18b).

Good News! A Positive Witness

The name Gospelizers promotes and preserves the **positive witness** of the Church, for the Christian message of God's grace, power, peace, and joy for fallen humanity is most optimistic! Just as "Gospel" means "Good News," so Gospelizers indicates those who announce/bring/show Good News. Gospelizers are like "angels" bearing God's Good News in bad times.[40] These are bad times. Yet, the present darkness and spirit of hopelessness offers a great chance for Gospelizers to bring heaven's best news to a hurting humanity in dire straits. As literally translated, Romans 10:15b uplifts the good news of Christ's messengers with intensity: "How beautiful are the feet of *Gospelizers* of **good things**!"[41]

In our witness, despite the sad state of world affairs, the focus of the Church must stay positively centered on Good News from God about Jesus. We proclaim Christ's coming, His redemption, liberation, deliverance, peace, blessings, and free gift of eternal life to every believer among all people in the world (cf. Mark 16:15).[42] We have a wonderful message from God — Christ the Lord, our Savior has come into the world! He lived and died for our sins, and was buried and rose back to life for our justification before God! The Good News is that Christ reveals His resurrection and saving presence to everyone who repents and believes the Gospel (cf. Mark 1:15).[43] Christ will not turn away anyone who comes to Him, and their belief in Him will never disappoint them.[44] That's Good News!

Jesus is always Good News! He is especially Good News for those who are down and out or victimized and marginalized. Jesus said to them,

> [28] "Come to me, all you that are weary and are carrying heavy burdens, and I will give you rest. [29] Take my yoke upon you, and learn from me; for I am gentle and humble in heart, and you will find rest for your souls. [30] For my yoke is easy, and my burden is light" (Matthew 11:28-30).

The truth and grace and power and salvation and peace and joy and freedom and help and everything about Jesus is *great news!* In our witness in the world, we must remind the Church continually that our faith-relationship with Jesus is always Good News. Understanding our Christian identity as Gospelizers goes a long way toward keeping our Good News message upbeat.

A Holistic Witness and Mission

The name *Gospelizers* brings together into one concise term **the holistic nature of believers' witness.** An authentic and holistic Christian witness and mission show up in **good words**, in **gracious works**, and in **great workings** of God (all powerful and miraculous). Communication, demonstration, and transformation demonstrate a true Gospel witness. Gospelizers (the name and the persons who minister) captures all three in one, leaving no room for an unspiritual dichotomy that diminishes action or results in favor of an exclusively spoken emphasis. Using Gospelizers in our conversation and teaching facilitates Christian dialogue. Implicitly Gospelizers are holistic, and need only be identified to connote this meaning and their nature.

"Disciple," "apostle," "evangelist," and "missionary," express varied aspects of a Christian witness for Christ. Though "evangelist" and "missionary" come close, neither term (as they are often used), captures fully the holistic gist and essence of the Christian witness and mission as does Gospelizer.[45]

By contrast, Gospelizers cuts to the chase, gets to the heart of the holistic Christian witness. Like none other, Gospelizers highlights the Church's proactive and full mission of bearing Good News in the world in the name of Christ our Redeemer. Gospelizers provide content, not just activity. As followers of Christ we announce, we live, and we miraculously manifest the Gospel in its holistic nature. The Apostle Paul wrote the following words in a testimonial report of his gospelizing: "...I have **fully** proclaimed the good news of Christ [literally, *I have fulfilled,* or *accomplished thoroughly,* or *brought to an end the gospel of Christ*]"[46] (Romans 15:19b, emphasis mine, cf. vv. 14-21). When fully and authentically gospelized, the Gospel effectually addresses all issues of life. True Gospelizers manifest this holistic mission.

A Mission Focus

Using Gospelizers to identify Christ's followers **keeps the Church focused in a mission-minded mode of operation**. The Church's mission is to go out, not to become ingrown. Several Biblical names describe the followers of Christ and our witness in the world. Each name serves its own important purpose. However, Gospelizers is more mission-oriented, and thus raises a mission consciousness.

Followers of "The Way"[47] point to the sole and unique Saviorhood of Christ Jesus, and of our living pattern in the Lord. We are on "the way" to glory and to heaven, and we are committed to "the way" of living taught by our Lord. As "Christians"[48] (a disparaging label for members of the church at Antioch), we are a people "of Christ," "of the Anointed One," "of the Messiah." We are "fanatics," so to speak, of Christ; "Christ is our life," we belong to Christ, have the nature of the Anointed One, and are devoted and "addicted" to Him in all things. "Disciples"[49] are "learners." Of course, the emphasis here is on adhering to the teachings and lifestyle of our Teacher. We are faithful followers of our Lord. When we are called "Saints,"[50] our holiness is brought to the table. We are "holy ones," having been cleansed from our sins, and are continually endeavoring to live a life of sanctification and righteousness, personal and public. We are ever seeking to gain freedom from the power of sin in our ungodly experience, and to manifest spirituality in all of life. As "Believers"[51] we have placed implicit faith in the trustworthiness of God. We live by faith in order to please God, and to receive all the blessings of His grace that He has promised to deliver to those who trust Him. As "Children of God" and "Brothers" and "Sisters,"[52] we recognize the spiritual relationship we share with our heavenly Father and with one another in Christ. Through being "born again" ("born from above," cf. John 3:3, 7) God has become our Father in a way we did not know before we took Jesus as our Savior. We are God's sons and daughters. We are family. We belong to each other. As "Ministers"[53] we are servants. Under God, Jesus came to serve humanity. So do we. Our Lord has commanded us to righteously serve one another and humanity. We are "Soldiers"[54] because we are on the battlefield for our Lord. Our warfare is against the satanic powers of darkness, and the weapons of our warfare are spiritual. We are in God's army, and must fight if we would reign with Christ. Closer to defining our mission is "Witnesses," a term that describes more of a function than a name, clearly implying some of the mission activity being encouraged.[55]

Thus, followers of Christ are variously identified as people of "The Way," "Christians," "Disciples," "Saints," "Believers," "Children of God," "Brothers" or "Sisters," "Ministers," "Soldiers," and "Witnesses."

Identifying ourselves as Gospelizers emphasizes our mission of spreading the "Good News" of Christ to those who by virtue of sin are lost without Christ. We *gospelize* so that they may hear, believe, and call on the name of the Lord for His salvation. For the Word proclaims in Romans 10:13-15,

> [13] For, "Everyone who calls on the name of the Lord shall be saved." [14] But how are they to call on one in whom they have not believed? And how are they to believe in one of whom they have never heard? And how are they to hear without someone to proclaim [*kerusso*][56] him? [15] And how are they to proclaim [*kerusso*] him unless they are sent? As it is written, *"How beautiful are the feet of those who bring good news [Gospelizers]!"*[57] (emphasis mine)

The engine that continually drives believers' great endeavors—the unique, essential, central, and motivating mission of the Church—is our announcing Christ's coming to humanity, with His forgiveness and redemption from sin and its aftermath. This holistic witness involves gospelizing the Gospel and is the Church's utmost calling. Identifying followers of Christ as Gospelizers continually reminds the Church of our mission—to go forth to a fallen and lost humanity, bearing the eternal Gospel of God's love, pardon from sin, redemption,[58] call to community and righteousness, and the blessings which flow from God's great salvation.

The Recommended Name-of-Choice

In summary, the following shows what we see and gain by using Gospelizers as our name of choice for messengers of God who spread the good word of Jesus in witness on His redeeming mission.

"Gospelizers"

The recommended name-of-choice that best identifies
God-sent messengers whose holistic witness brings
the Good News of Christ's presence and
redeeming mission to humanity.
"Gospelizers" shows clarity and force,
and immediately signifies...

1. *"Gospel"* –The essential and central revealed truth and content of the Christian message.

2. *Jesus Christ* – The Author and Subject of the Gospel and the four *Gospels*.

3. *"Good News"* – The positive message bringing hope and help to all people fraught with "bad news."

4. *A Holistic Witness and Mission* – Comprising good words, gracious works, and great workings of God!

5. *A Mission Focus* – Compelling the Church to proactively move out into our world, bringing forth Christ and spreading His blessings of salvation.

5

Identity, Mission, and Witness

> *The Call:*
> • **Study carefully the paradigm of Gospelizers.**

Let us now pursue a deeper understanding of Gospelizers. The argument for the identity, mission, and witness of Gospelizers is anchored in the model of Jesus in His ministry, in the teachings and commands of Jesus' Word, and in the teaching and experience of the early Church.

Luke 8:1-3
The Mission of Jesus, and The Twelve,
Some Women, and Many Others with Him

Identity

By insight from the Holy Spirit I gained a greater appreciation of the idea of Gospelizers while preparing a sermon manuscript on Luke 8:1-3.[59] Here are the verses:

> [1] Soon afterwards he [Jesus] went on through cities and villages, **proclaiming and bringing the good news** of the kingdom of God. The twelve were with him, [2] as

well as some women who had been cured of evil spirits and infirmities: Mary, called Magdalene, from whom seven demons had gone out, 3 and Joanna, the wife of Herod's steward Chuza, and Susanna, and many others, who provided for them out of their resources (emphasis mine).

The phrase in verse 1, "proclaiming and bringing the good news," is quite powerful. Underlying its translation are two Greek terms: *kerusso* and *euangelizo*. Translating this verse, different versions render these two terms in the following manner:

"proclaiming the good news" (NIV)
"preaching and announcing the Gospel" (Intl. N.T.)
"proclaiming the good news" (CEV)
"preaching and proclaiming the good news" (KJV SB)
"announce the Good News" (NLT)
"preaching and showing the glad tidings" (KJV)
"preaching and bringing the glad tidings" (NKJV)
"proclaiming and bringing the good news" (NRSV)

Taken together, Luke's Gospel words describe the witness/mission campaign of Jesus.[60] *Kerusso* means to "proclaim openly with authority" (as a herald). *Euangelizo* means "to bring or announce (as an angel would tell) the good news or the Gospel."[61] *Euangelizo* is the verb that is translated as gospelize. The messengers who announce the "good news" are literally Gospelizers. The noun form of the message or content is *euangelion,* or Gospel.[62]

Actually, *euangelizo* means more than simply telling or announcing a good word. *Euangelizo* also connotes *doing* or *practicing* the Good News. We gain this understanding by studying the term's rich use in the New Testament Scriptures. "...Jesus' ministry was portrayed as a proclaiming of the good news by speech and deed."[63] As a Gospelizer, Jesus was a performer. He practiced the action of doing good works.

When preaching, Peter gave a summary of Jesus' ministry using the word *euangelizo* in Acts 10:36. He said that God was **"preaching [gospelizing] peace by Jesus Christ"** (emphasis mine). Describing this *"gospelizing,"* Peter went on to say,

> [38] how God anointed Jesus of Nazareth with the Holy Spirit and with power; how **he went about doing good** and healing all who were oppressed with the devil, for God was with him. [39] We are witnesses to **all that he did** both in Judea and in Jerusalem" (Acts 10:38-39, emphasis mine).

Further, two of Jesus' disciples testified about His life. They said,

> "Jesus of Nazareth...was a prophet **mighty in deed and word** before God and all the people" (Luke 24:19, emphasis mine).

In other words, Gospelizers bring the Good News of Christ; they "speak and act," "tell and show," "talk and walk."[64] And they do this gospelizing personally and as a collective community.

Yet, the meaning of *euangelizo* offers a third, deeper level. *Euangelizo* also carries the force of *impartation*, "proclamation with full authority and power. Signs and wonders accompany the evangelical message. They belong together..."[65]

This means that announcing and demonstrating the Gospel is done with such **power and authority** that the richer blessings of this spoken word and its practical applications are imparted, or passed on, to the hearers. This results in manifesting or revealing the **miraculous workings** of God.[66] In this impartation, the hearers are granted a share or portion of the Gospel. They are bestowed with salvation, peace, power, healing, deliverance, freedom, a sense of social righteousness and justice—whatever the

Gospel graciously and powerfully effects in their experience at the time.[67]

Holistic Witness and Mission

Consequently, the Gospelizers' message **effects** (more than *affects*)[68] an evident, miraculous change in the life-situation of the hearers. *Effectual results* are attained through the proclamation and performance of the Word. Thus, the meaning of *euangelizo* covers three areas of Christian witness: *the words, practices,* and *outcomes* of the messengers' ministry. The Scriptures reveal this richer meaning.

In Luke 8:1-3, Jesus, accompanied by the twelve disciples/apostles and certain other women, did mission work in every city and town they visited. The specific women who journeyed with Jesus and the twelve were "**Mary**, called Magdalene, from whom seven demons had gone out, and **Joanna**, the wife of Herod's steward Chuza, and **Susanna**, and **many others**…" (vv. 2, 3, emphasis mine). Based on a holistic understanding of gospelize *(euangelizo)*, Jesus and those with Him gave a three-fold witness in their mission.

1. By their *good words* they gave witness to the Good News of Jesus through preaching, heralding, proclaiming, announcing, telling the Gospel;

2. By their *gracious works* they gave witness to the Good News of Jesus by showing, bringing, doing, demonstrating the Gospel;[69]

3. By their *great workings* of God's power they gave witness to the Good News of Jesus by manifesting, imparting, effecting the Gospel.

During Jesus' witnessing campaign accompanied by His followers, they were gospelizing the kingdom of God! They were *gospelizing* the presence of the Lord—King Jesus—and the authority and blessings of His theocratic reign.[70] The reign of Christ manifests itself in the heart, life, and all human affairs. Jesus is King of kings, and Lord of all.

Outcomes and Effects are Important

A holistic Gospel mission includes words, practices, and *outcomes*. Among the three elements of gospelizing the *outcomes ("great workings")* are most important. Those "women who had been cured of evil spirits and infirmities" (Luke 8:2a) by Jesus went witnessing with Him and His disciples in the cities and towns. As they went, we might naturally assume that their Gospel witness about Jesus would include their own personal testimony of the deliverance and healing Jesus had already done for them. Jesus had **effected** a mighty work of deliverance in the lives of these women. So in their witness they would naturally expect that the same miraculous results of Jesus' work in their own lives could *and would* be done for others. Jesus would impart and work the blessings of His Gospel in the lives of others who responded with the faith of those women.

Gospelizing runs its full course when the announcement of Jesus' presence produces powerful, miraculous, consequential, and resulting effects. The **impartation** of the Gospelizers' announcement demonstrates gospelizing at its best. The witness of *Gospelizers* is not limited to a spoken word and an acted upon word. It is also an *effectual word*.

Appearing after His resurrection, Jesus spoke the following words to His disciples:

¹⁵" ...Go into all the world and proclaim *[kerusso]*[71] the

good news to the whole creation. [16] The one who believes and is baptized will be saved; but the one who does not believe will be condemned. [17] And **these signs** will accompany those who believe: by using my name they will cast out demons; they will speak in new tongues; [18] they will pick up snakes in their hands, and if they drink any deadly thing, it will not hurt them; they will lay their hands on the sick, and they will recover" (Mark 16:15-18, emphasis mine).

The Gospel writer Mark affirmed these words of Jesus by writing:

[19] So then the Lord Jesus, after he had spoken to them, was taken up into heaven and sat down at the right hand of God. [20] And they went out and proclaimed *[kerusso]*[72] the good news everywhere, while **the Lord worked** with them and confirmed the message by the **signs** that accompanied it (Mark 16:19-20, emphasis mine).

The reference in the verses above to certain "signs" and workings of God are an indication of the "effectual word" of Gospelizers. As Gospelizers fulfill their mission, they find that God Himself is gospelizing with them and confirming their message.[73] *Preaching, practicing,* and *"signing"* compose the complete witness of Gospelizers. See the following chart and cross-references.[74]

The Holistic Witness of *Gospelizers*		
WORDS	**PRACTICES**	**OUTCOMES**
The Spoken Word	The Acted Word	The Effectual Word
Good Words	Gracious Works	Great Workings
Proclaiming	Performing	Imparting
Announcing	Living	Manifesting
Preaching	Practicing	"Signing"
Communication	Demonstration	Transformation

Description of Holistic Witness

Thus we have established the holistic witness and mission of Gospelizers as revealed in *euangelizo*. They are holistic for they are co-workers with God; they serve with Christ on His redeeming mission in the world. They are holistic for they are inclusive of all Christ's messengers, men and women. They are holistic because their gospelizing encompasses words, works, and miraculous workings of God. They effectually serve the totality of human need: body, spirit, and soul. Persons and societies are healed and made "whole" by the imparted results of gospelizing. They are holistic because their gracious and righteous works are done personally and collectively; and they minister to individuals as well as "cities and villages." They are holistic because they gospelize God's kingdom—His new social order—wherein Christ the Lord reigns in the hearts, lives, and total affairs of humanity. The sphere of Christ's gospelized kingdom transcends and supercedes the system of this world, and provides a new community—a community of fellowship in the Gospel[75]—for all who place their wholehearted trust in Him. This is the holistic witness and mission of Gospelizers.

Gospelizing IS (Review and Preview)

As our understanding of Gospelizers is being formed, it is well to pause and reflect on certain implications of our definition. Some of these points have already been covered, others will be explained later.

• **Gospelizing is both a collective and individual ministry** (cf. Luke 8:1-3; Acts 8:1-4; Philippians 1:28ff.; Romans 10:15b). Gospelizing by believers should model the mission campaign of Jesus who included His messengers with Him on His mission. Jesus also organized and commissioned gospelizing teams (e.g., two by two). Gospelizing is more than an individual Christian responsibility. It is a Church responsibility, and an opportunity to bear a strong collective witness to Jesus in the harvest-fields (see chapter 12). The Apostle Paul wrote to the church at Philippi, exhorting them to unity in gospelizing:

> [27] Only, live your life in a manner worthy of the gospel of Christ, so that, whether I come and see you or am absent and hear about you, I will know that you are standing firm in one spirit, striving side by side with one mind for the faith of the gospel, [28] and are in no way intimidated by your opponents (Philippians 1:27-28a).

• **Gospelizing is holistic** (as stated above). We reemphasize two aspects of this dimension. First, gospelizing manifests "gracious works" of personal and collective righteousness for individuals, groups, and societies. The driving force for these gracious works is the salvation imperative. There is more than a single reason for gospelizing gracious works. We do gracious works for individuals and groups because we love them and are compassionate toward their personal needs. We do gracious works in society because we desire to correct systemic problems that cause persons and groups to suffer. Utmost, we do gracious works because we desire to bring the eternal salvation of Christ to persons, their households, entire communities, and every nation. The salvation imperative operates at the center of Gospelizers' gracious works.

Second, gospelizing is holistic because it imparts "great workings" of God. Gospelizing performs the miraculous, an unmatched Christ-anointed contribution to the well-being of humanity. With Christ, believers as spiritually endowed individuals and as members of the Body of Christ perform miracles. Miracles are gracious works of a supernatural and spiritual character. In the Name of Jesus, Gospelizers heal and deliver, perform the improbable, and bring about the impossible. Gospelizers pray, and God answers our prayers with many "wonders." These "signs" also point to Christ and the salvation found only in Him.

- **Gospelizing is a substantive ministry that calls sinners to respond in a wholehearted way to Christ's salvation invitation.** There are some "evangelistic" methods and approaches that leave much to be desired in this area, especially in the call to repentance. The true call of the Gospel requires of salvation seekers that they "deny themselves and take up their cross daily and follow" Christ (Luke 9:23). The Apostle Paul, gospelized by Jesus on the Damascus Road, testified for Christ's sake: "I have suffered the loss of all things" (Philippians 3:8b). The apostle also declared, "For Christ did not send me to baptize but to proclaim the gospel *[to gospelize]*" (1 Corinthians 1:17a), indicating that gospelizing is not a "numbers game." Jesus commanded one man, "Let the dead bury their own dead; but as for you, go and proclaim the kingdom of God" (Luke 9:60). True conversion manifests itself in repentance, a changed life of righteousness and holiness, and a commitment to serving Christ in the world. Genuine converts begin to live "life in a manner worthy of the Gospel of Christ" (Philippians 1:27a).

• **Gospelizing is "*Koinonia*-izing."** Apart from the impartation of salvation and its blessings to those who confess, believe, and take Christ the Lord as their Savior, bringing the Church of Christ to the lost is the greatest good work of Gospelizers (Matthew 16:18ff.; Acts 9:31; 14:23). Later we will highlight the emphasis Gospelizers must place on organizing the new community of Christ, the *Koinonia*, in the harvest-fields of communities in the world (see chapter 11). The Church's zeal for gospelizing through *Koinonia*-izing ought to take center stage. *Koinonia*-izing ministry must rival both the infusion of Christians serving Christ in public areas, and the developing of parachurch ministries and institutions. Gospelizing demands that our churches become proficient in the practice of organizing other churches as a witness for Christ that serves the needs of new converts, and perpetuates the Church throughout the world.

• **Gospelizing is a challenge, by its very nature, to all ungodly and evil systems.** Christ challenged an oppressive socio-economic system when He gospelized the Jubilee (cf. Luke 4:18-19). Christ implicitly challenged the Roman political system when He and His disciples gospelized "the kingdom of God" (Luke 8:1; 9:2; 10:8). Christ challenged a repressive and hypocritical religious system and its leaders when He gospelized with divine authority in the temple at Jerusalem (Luke 20:1-8). The early Church followed the pattern of Christ and defied their religious leaders who sought to intimidate and prohibit their gospelizing in Christ's name: They said, "We must obey God rather than any human authority" (Acts 5:29b). The Gospel of gospelizing takes on the struggle against satanic and evil forces manifested in godless human authority and systems. As the Church reaches out with gospelizing, the Church will confront, engage, withstand, and consistently overcome the very "gates of hell."

Recovering "Gospelizers" and Renewing Our Witness

At times believers and churches are criticized for our inability to have a greater impact in the world for Christ. Some of the criticism is justified. Christ's messengers should be doing much more and much better than we are. What is the reason for our impotence? Perhaps the answer is found in our shallow understanding and weak application of Christ's Gospel and His mission of gospelizing. Much of our impotence in effecting our world for Christ is traceable to our failure to grasp and exploit for righteous purposes what it really means for us to be Christ's Gospelizers.

In many ways, as believers and churches we are disappointing Christ, spoiling the hope He has placed in us. We have lost focus of our true identity and witness as Christ's gospelizing messengers. In matters of mission we have insulated ourselves in mediocrity and normality. We are "lukewarm" (cf. Revelation 3:16). As believers we have neutralized our witness, and dissipated our spiritual strengths by maintaining an "outward form of godliness but denying its power" (2 Timothy 3:5a). Consequently, Christ's followers and our churches are more impotent for effecting substantial change in our societies than many of us would care to confess. Our impotence has shamed the Lord's miraculous Name: Jesus, salvation.

Yet, there is a corrective: we can recover "Gospelizers" and renew our witness in the mission of Christ. Our study of gospelizing predicates itself on a spiritual truism: **when we know Christ better, we'll do Christ better.** So,

> [12] ...work out your own salvation with fear and trembling; [13] for it is God who is at work in you, enabling you both to will and to work for his good pleasure (Philippians 2:12b-13).

> I can do all things through him [Christ] who strengthens me (Philippians 4:13).

6

Gospelizer Jesus and Other Models

The Call:
- **Study carefully the paradigm of Gospelizers.**

The following Scripture passages highlight the experience of *Gospelizers.* We begin with Jesus[76] and proceed to accentuate His followers.

GOSPELIZER JESUS

The Preeminent Paradigm

Jesus Gospelizes the "Jubilee" to the Poor
Luke 4:16-22

> 16 When he came to Nazareth, where he had been brought up, he went to the synagogue on the Sabbath day, as was his custom. He stood up to read, 17 and the scroll of the prophet Isaiah was given to him. He unrolled the scroll and found the place where it was

written: 18 "The Spirit of the Lord is upon me, because he has anointed me to bring good news *[to gospelize]* to the poor. He has sent me to proclaim release to the captives and recovery of sight to the blind, to let the oppressed go free, 19 to proclaim the year of the Lord's favor." 20 And he rolled up the scroll, gave it back to the attendant, and sat down. The eyes of all in the synagogue were fixed on him. 21 Then he began to say to them, "Today this scripture has been fulfilled in your hearing." 22 All spoke well of him and were amazed at the gracious words that came from his mouth. They said, "Is not this Joseph's son?"

Jesus' Gospelizing is in Demand
Luke 4:40-44

40 As the sun was setting, all those who had any who were sick with various kinds of diseases brought them to him; and he laid his hands on each of them and cured them. 41 Demons also came out of many, shouting, "You are the Son of God!" But he rebuked them and would not allow them to speak, because they knew that he was the Messiah. 42 At daybreak he departed and went into a deserted place. And the crowds were looking for him, and when they reached him, they wanted to prevent him from leaving them. 43 But he said to them, "I must proclaim the good news of *[gospelize]* the kingdom of God to the other cities also; for I was sent for this purpose." 44 So he continued proclaiming the message *[kerusso]*[77] in the synagogues of Judea.

Jesus Gospelizes for John the Baptizer[78]
Luke 7:18-23 (cf. Matthew 11:2ff.)

18 The disciples of John reported all these things to him. So John summoned two of his disciples 19 and sent them to the Lord to ask, "Are you the one who is to come, or are we to wait for another?" 20 When the men

had come to him, they said, "John the Baptist has sent us to you to ask, 'Are you the one who is to come, or are we to wait for another?'" 21 Jesus had just then cured many people of diseases, plagues, and evil spirits, and had given sight to many who were blind. 22 And he answered them, "Go and tell John what you have seen and heard: the blind receive their sight, the lame walk, the lepers are cleansed, the deaf hear, the dead are raised, the poor have good news brought to them *[are gospelized]*. 23 And blessed is anyone who takes no offense at me."

Jesus Gospelizes with the "Twelve" and Many Women
Luke 8:1-3

1 Soon afterwards he [Jesus] went on through cities and villages, **proclaiming** *[kerusso]*[79] **and bringing the good news** *[gospelizing]* of the kingdom of God. The twelve were with him, 2 as well as some women who had been cured of evil spirits and infirmities: Mary, called Magdalene, from whom seven demons had gone out, 3 and Joanna, the wife of Herod's steward Chuza, and Susanna, and many others, who provided for them out of their resources (emphasis mine).

Jesus' Gospelizing Replaces the Law and Prophets
Luke 16:16

The law and the prophets were in effect until John came; since then the good news of the kingdom of God is proclaimed *[is gospelized]*, and everyone tries to enter it by force.

Mark 1:14-15

14 Now after John was arrested, Jesus came to Galilee, proclaiming *[kerusso]*[80] the good news of God, 15 and saying, "The time is fulfilled, and the kingdom of God has come near; repent, and believe in the good news."

Jesus Gospelizes in Galilee
Matthew 4:23-25

23 Jesus went throughout Galilee, teaching in their synagogues and proclaiming *[kerusso]*81 *[gospelizing]* the good news of the kingdom and curing every disease and every sickness among the people. 24 So his fame spread throughout all Syria, and they brought to him all the sick, those who were afflicted with various diseases and pains, demoniacs, epileptics, and paralytics, and he cured them. 25 And great crowds followed him from Galilee, the Decapolis, Jerusalem, Judea, and from beyond the Jordan.

Jesus Gospelizes the Shepherdless Crowds
Matthew 9:35-38

35 Then Jesus went about all the cities and villages, teaching in their synagogues, and proclaiming *[kerusso]*82 the good news of the kingdom, and curing every disease and every sickness. 36 When he saw the crowds, he had compassion for them, because they were harassed and helpless, like sheep without a shepherd. 37 Then he said to his disciples, "The harvest is plentiful, but the laborers are few; 38 therefore ask the Lord of the harvest to send out laborers into his harvest."

Jesus Gospelizes with Authority in the Temple
Luke 20:1-2

1 One day, as he was teaching the people in the temple and telling the good news *[gospelizing]*, the chief priests and scribes came with the elders 2 and said to him, "Tell us, by what authority are you doing these things? Who is it who gave you this authority?"83

Matthew 21:14

The blind and the lame came to him in the temple, and he cured them.

Jesus Came Gospelizing Peace to All
Ephesians 2:17

> So he came and proclaimed *[gospelized]* peace to you who were far off and peace to those who were near.

John the Baptist Gospelizes[84]
Luke 3:18

> So, with many other exhortations, he proclaimed the good news *[gospelized]* to the people.

Commissioned by Jesus, the Twelve Disciples/Apostles
*   Gospelize*
Luke 9:1-2, 6 (cf. Matthew 10:1ff.; Mark 6:7ff.)

> [1] Then Jesus called the twelve together and gave them power and authority over all demons and to cure diseases, [2] and he sent them out to proclaim *[kerusso]*[85] the kingdom of God and to heal. [6] They departed and went through the villages, bringing the good news *[gospelizing]* and curing diseases everywhere.

The Commission of the Seventy and the Gospelizing
*   Authority of Jesus' Name*
Luke 10:1, 8-9, 17-20

> [1] After this the Lord appointed seventy others and sent them on ahead of him in pairs to every town and place where he himself intended to go. [8] [Jesus said,] "Whenever you enter a town and its people welcome you, eat what is set before you; [9] cure the sick who are there, and say to them, 'The kingdom of God has come near to you.'" [17] The seventy returned with joy, saying, **"Lord, in your name even the demons submit to us!"** [18] He said to them, "I watched Satan fall from heaven like a flash of lightning. [19] See, I have given you authority to tread on snakes and scorpions, and over all

the power of the enemy; and nothing will hurt you. [20] Nevertheless, do not rejoice at this, that the spirits submit to you, but rejoice that your names are written in heaven" (emphasis mine).

The Apostles Gospelized
Acts 5:12-20, 25, 28, 40-42

[12] Now many signs and wonders were done among the people through the apostles. And they were all together in Solomon's Portico. [13] None of the rest dared to join them, but the people held them in high esteem. [14] Yet more than ever believers were added to the Lord, great numbers of both men and women, [15] so that they even carried out the sick into the streets, and laid them on cots and mats, in order that Peter's shadow might fall on some of them as he came by. [16] A great number of people would also gather from the towns around Jerusalem, bringing the sick and those tormented by unclean spirits, and they were all cured. [17] Then the high priest took action; he and all who were with him (that is, the sect of the Sadducees), being filled with jealousy, [18] arrested the apostles and put them in the public prison. [19] But during the night an angel of the Lord opened the prison doors, brought them out, and said, [20] "Go, stand in the temple and tell the people the whole message about this life." [25] Then someone arrived and announced [to the high priest], "Look, the men whom you put in prison are standing in the temple and teaching the people!" [28] ...[The high priest said to the apostles,] "We gave you strict orders not to teach in this name, yet here you have filled Jerusalem with your teaching and you are determined to bring this man's blood on us." [40] and when they [the ruling council] had called in the apostles, they had them flogged. Then they ordered them not to speak in the name of Jesus, and let them go. [41] As they [the apostles] left the

council, they rejoiced that they were considered worthy to suffer dishonor for the sake of the name. ⁴²And every day in the temple and at home they did not cease to teach and proclaim *[gospelize]* Jesus as the Messiah.⁸⁶

Hebrews 2:3-4

³how can we escape if we neglect so great a salvation? It was declared at first through the Lord, and it was attested to us by those who heard him, ⁴**while God added his testimony by signs and wonders and various miracles, and by gifts of the Holy Spirit,** distributed according to his will (emphasis mine).

The Persecuted [Terrorized] Church Gospelizes
Acts 8:1-5

¹And Saul approved of their killing him [Stephen]. That day a severe persecution began against the church in Jerusalem, and all except the apostles were scattered throughout the countryside of Judea and Samaria. ²Devout men buried Stephen and made loud lamentation over him. ³But Saul was ravaging the church by entering house after house; dragging off both men and women, he committed them to prison. ⁴Now those who were scattered went from place to place, proclaiming *[gospelizing]* the word. ⁵Philip went down to the city of Samaria and proclaimed *[kerusso]*⁸⁷ the Messiah to them.

Philip the Gospelizer, Peter and John Gospelize
Acts 8:6-8, 12, 25, 35, 40

⁶The crowds with one accord listened eagerly to what was said by Philip, hearing and seeing the signs that he did, ⁷for unclean spirits, crying with loud shrieks, came out of many who were possessed; and many others who were paralyzed or lame were cured. ⁸So there was great joy in that city. ¹²But when they believed Philip, who was proclaiming the good news *[gospelizing]*

about the kingdom of God and the name of Jesus Christ, they were baptized, both men and women. [25] Now after Peter and John had testified and spoken the word of the Lord, they returned to Jerusalem, proclaiming the good news *[gospelizing]* to many villages of the Samaritans. [35] Then Philip began to speak, and starting with this scripture, he proclaimed *[gospelized]* to him [the Ethiopian Eunuch] the good news about Jesus. [40] But Philip found himself at Azotus, and as he was passing through the region, he proclaimed the good news *[gospelized]* to all the towns until he came to Caesarea.[88]

Acts 21:8-9

[8] The next day we left and came to Caesarea; and we went into the house of Philip the evangelist *[Gospelizer]*, one of the seven, and stayed with him. [9] He had four unmarried daughters who had the gift of prophecy.

Peter Gospelizes the Peace of God to the Household of Cornelius
Acts 10:34-43

[34] Then Peter began to speak to them: "I truly understand that God shows no partiality, [35] but in every nation anyone who fears him and does what is right is acceptable to him. [36] You know the message he sent to the people of Israel, preaching *[gospelizing]* peace by Jesus Christ—he is Lord of all. [37] That message spread throughout Judea, beginning in Galilee after the baptism that John announced: [38] how God anointed Jesus of Nazareth with the Holy Spirit and with power; how he went about doing good and healing all who were oppressed by the devil, for God was with him. [39] We are witnesses to all that he did both in Judea and in Jerusalem. They put him to death by hanging him on a

tree; ⁴⁰ but God raised him on the third day and allowed him to appear, ⁴¹ not to all the people but to us who were chosen by God as witnesses, and who ate and drank with him after he rose from the dead. ⁴² He commanded us to preach to the people and to testify that he is the one ordained by God as judge of the living and the dead. ⁴³ All the prophets testify about him that everyone who believes in him receives forgiveness of sins through his name."

Men of Cyprus and Cyrene Gospelize among the Hellenists
Acts 11:19-21

¹⁹ Now those who were scattered because of the persecution that took place over Stephen traveled as far as Phoenicia, Cyprus, and Antioch, and they spoke the word to no one except Jews. ²⁰ But among them were some men of Cyprus and Cyrene who, on coming to Antioch, spoke to the Hellenists also, proclaiming [*gospelizing*] the Lord Jesus. ²¹The hand of the Lord was with them, and a great number became believers and turned to the Lord.

Paul and Barnabas Gospelize
Acts 13:26-35

²⁶"My brothers, you descendants of Abraham's family, and others who fear God, to us the message of this salvation has been sent. ²⁷ Because the residents of Jerusalem and their leaders did not recognize him or understand the words of the prophets that are read every sabbath, they fulfilled those words by condemning him. ²⁸ Even though they found no cause for a sentence of death, they asked Pilate to have him killed. ²⁹ When they had carried out everything that was written about him, they took him down from the tree and laid him in a tomb. ³⁰ But God raised him from the dead; ³¹ and for many days he appeared to those who

came up with him from Galilee to Jerusalem, and they are now his witnesses to the people. 32 And we bring you the good news *[we gospelize to you]* that what God promised to our ancestors 33 he has fulfilled for us, their children, by raising Jesus; as also it is written in the second psalm, 'You are my Son; today I have begotten you.' 34 As to his raising him from the dead, no more to return to corruption, he has spoken in this way, 'I will give you the holy promises made to David.' 35 Therefore he has also said in another psalm, 'You will not let your Holy One experience corruption.'"

Acts 14:1-7

1 The same thing occurred in Iconium, where Paul and Barnabas went into the Jewish synagogue and spoke in such a way that a great number of both Jews and Greeks became believers. 2 But the unbelieving Jews stirred up the Gentiles and poisoned their minds against the brothers. 3 So they remained for a long time, speaking boldly for the Lord, **who testified to the word of his grace by granting signs and wonders to be done through them.** 4 But the residents of the city were divided; some sided with the Jews, and some with the apostles. 5 And when an attempt was made by both Gentiles and Jews, with their rulers, to mistreat them and to stone them, 6 the apostles learned of it and fled to Lystra and Derbe, cities of Lycaonia, and to the surrounding country; 7 and there they continued proclaiming the good news *[continued gospelizing]* (emphasis mine).

Acts 14:8-10, 15

8 In Lystra there was a man sitting who could not use his feet and had never walked, for he had been crippled from birth. 9 He listened to Paul as he was speaking. And Paul, looking at him intently and seeing that he had faith to be healed, 10 said in a loud

voice, "Stand upright on your feet." And the man sprang up and began to walk. [15][Paul and Barnabas said,] "Friends, why are you doing this? We are mortals just like you, and we bring you good news *[gospelize]*, that you should turn from these worthless things to the living God, who made the heaven and the earth and the sea and all that is in them."

The Apostle Paul Gospelizes[89]
Romans 1:11, 15-16

[11] For I am longing to see you so that I may share with you some spiritual gift to strengthen you — [15] — hence my eagerness to proclaim the gospel *[to gospelize]* to you also who are in Rome. [16] For I am not ashamed of the gospel; it is the power of God for salvation to everyone who has faith, to the Jew first and also to the Greek.

Romans 15:17-21

[17] In Christ Jesus, then, I have reason to boast of my work for God. [18] For I will not venture to speak of anything except what Christ has accomplished through me to win obedience from the Gentiles, **by word and deed, [19] by the power of signs and wonders, by the power of the Spirit of God,** so that from Jerusalem and as far around as Illyricum I have fully proclaimed the good news of Christ. [20] Thus I make it my ambition to proclaim the good news *[to gospelize]*, not where Christ has already been named, so that I do not build on someone else's foundation, [21] but as it is written, "Those who have never been told of him shall see, and those who have never heard of him shall understand" (emphasis mine).

2 Corinthians 12:12

The signs of a true apostle were performed among you with utmost patience, **signs and wonders and mighty works** (emphasis mine).

The Apostle Peter Gospelizes
1 Peter 1:25

> 25 "but the word of the Lord endures forever." That word is the good news that was announced *[That word was gospelized]* to you.

Paul Tells Timothy to Do the Work of a Gospelizer
2 Timothy 4:5

> As for you, always be sober, endure suffering, do the work of an evangelist *[a Gospelizer]*, carry out your ministry fully.

The Call:

• **Study carefully the paradigm of *"Gospelizers."***

Give serious attention to an in-depth study of *"Gospelizers"* in Biblical usage, with a view toward receiving this term as an identifying name of Christ's mission-minded messengers. This concept should receive careful Scriptural examination and reflection in both personal devotions and church instruction classes. Along with study, believers should offer prayers for wisdom, understanding, and obedience to God. In addition, believers should "talk-up" this mission among the saints and act on this word of Christ.

7

A Model Emerges Amidst Terror

The Early Church and
The Post-September 11th Church

"Now [having been **terrorized**] those who were
scattered went from place to place,
proclaiming *[gospelizing]* the word"
(Acts 8:4, emphasis mine).

The Call:
- **Gospelize with urgency and highest priority.**

The Early Church, The Post-September 11th Church
Acts 8:1-4

Nothing in recent times has so incisively demanded a
refocusing of the Church's agenda than the September 11,

2001 terrorist attacks in the United States, and their subsequent recurrences and socio-economic aftermaths. As never before, America's churches are faced with the compelling urgency to proclaim and impart the saving Gospel of Jesus Christ our Lord. The contemporary Church must replicate the actions of the earliest followers of Christ in the first century of the Christian faith. They, too, were affronted by a terrorizing situation.

In the life experience of the early believers, there arose a period of "severe persecution" against the Church in Jerusalem, sparked by Saul of Tarsus approving the stoning death of Stephen (cf. Acts 8:1, ca. 33 A.D.). A spirit of religious zealousness unmatched in his day possessed Saul (cf. Philippians 3:6; Acts 22:3-6). He spearheaded quite a disruptive and violently destructive move against the Church. With legal authority he invaded Christian church-households, attacked the believers, arrested and imprisoned both men and women, and gave his approval for their death sentences. Saul terrorized the Church with blasphemy, persecution, and violence (1 Timothy 1:13a).

But amidst such terrorizing the saints did not hide and entrench themselves, cowering for safety and security. The disciples of Jesus did not allow terror to curtail their movement or their mission. Instead, as the Scripture notes, the disciples of the "scattered" Church "went from place to place, **proclaiming the word**" (Acts 8:4, emphasis mine). They **"proclaimed the Messiah"** (cf. Acts 8:5, emphasis mine). These terrorized but courageous followers of Christ chose to decentralize and (literally) to "*gospelize*."[90]

With a sense of urgent abandonment, these believers changed their focus to extend their ministry. They forsook their present living situation. Hurriedly, they scattered and relocated into new areas. Surrendering self-centeredness and familiar surroundings, they put their personal lives and welfare at risk. Substituting one kind of trouble for another—amidst their own besetting issues of survival—these persecuted believers denied themselves. They became mobile, and freely gave themselves to the widespread witness of the Good News of Jesus Christ to save others. They proclaimed Jesus wherever they relocated. However, their witness was much more than a spoken word.

Inherent in the "Good News" message of these "terrorized" Gospel preachers was both an **acted word** and an **effectual word** from God. Their proclamation combined a **demonstration** and an **impartation** of God's grace, truth, and saving power. Their Gospel witness manifested **miraculous outcomes.** The Scripture variously refers to these results as "signs," "unclean spirits that...came out" (exorcisings); "cures," and "great miracles."[91] These followers of Christ experienced Jesus' delivering and healing "anointing" of the Spirit of the Lord.[92] Consequently, God used them to spread the many holistic blessings of the Gospel of God's salvation, wherever they went.

Agitated by the social pressures of a crisis, these terror-struck disciples of Christ became intensified Gospelizers. They announced Christ and His Good News in their world.[93] And they announced Christ in their words, in their works, and in their miraculous workings.

In His ministry, Jesus had already prepared His followers to become His special messengers. The Lord even prophesied their witness "to the ends of the earth" (Acts 1:8). When the Church was born, the coming of the Spirit to Christ's disciples on Pentecost gave them their initial thrust. Consequently, they gave a powerful witness to the Lord, but did so mainly in Jerusalem (Acts 2:1ff.).

As the disciples' witness effectively increased, so did their persecutions (cf. Acts 2:47; 3:6ff.; 4:1-4; 5:12-21; 6:8-15, 54ff.). Yet, as their persecutions increased, so did their *gospelizing* (cf. Acts 5:40-42). In this light, the "severe persecution" surrounding Stephen's death was simply an intensification of what had been happening to the disciples of Christ as they were associated with Jesus' crucifixion, and from near the very beginnings of the Church. Their response of bearing a greater witness was also an intensification. Thus, in a time of frightening persecution, the believers were transformed and abruptly emerged as the Gospelizers their Lord had already destined for them to become. They "scattered" and reached out with the Gospel in the name of Christ.

As followers of Christ, we also must quickly emerge as Gospelizers.

9-11-01, AIDS/HIV, and Other Terrorism

Since the destruction of September 11, 2001 the Church has responded in various ways to a widening crisis. Many called us to remembrance and reconciliation. Others urged revenge and retaliation. More prophetic voices called the Church (and the nation) to repentance.[94] It is always righteous for God's people to be responsive to crises, both at home and in our world. However, certain responses are better than others. How *should* the Church respond? What *ought* to become the *priority response* of Christ's followers to the recurring climate of terrorism in the world?

The chilling events of "9-11" serve as a "rise-up" call by Jesus to His slumbering and nauseatingly lukewarm Church. Our sovereign Lord has used this socio-economic "earthquake" to demand the attention of His Church, and to spur the people of God into our mission of gospelizing.

Arguably, the work of gospelizing should become the essential response of God's people. This mission is an urgent Biblical and spiritual response to the present climate of terrorism, the terrifying repercussions, and the tribulations besetting our already debilitating situations. This is especially true among Black believers and the African-descended faith-community.

Though many whites are shocked, terrorism is nothing new for Black folks, including Black believers in Christ.

We have been terrorized for hundreds of years. In the past and the present we have experienced much terror from the historical evils of white supremacy, racism. We have experienced the racial nature of raw evil in many dimensions of violence against African life: the MAAFA or "African Holocaust;"[95] the lynching of Black men, the raping of Black women, and the killing of innocent children in the South; the burning of crosses, bombing of churches, and other intimidation of Blacks by the Christian Knights of the Ku Klux Klan, Neo-Nazis, and other racial hate-groups; the unleashing of attack dogs and fire hoses on peace-minded civil rights marchers; the "criminalizing" of Black men (and increasingly young males and women) in prison and on death-row in numbers disproportionate to the general population. All this is terror. Black people know evil and terror.

To make matters worse, inasmuch as African-descended people share the identity of being American, we find ourselves the unwitting recipients of other physical, social, and economic terrorist acts. The flying bombs that struck the World Trade Center did not discriminate between Black and white. Terrorists' unleashing of "dirty bombs," biological and chemical agents such as anthrax, have not discriminated against racial or ethnic type. These are weapons of indiscriminate mass destruction. The intended targets of foreign terrorists' acts are racially non-specific, and are as geographically decentralized as the Al Queda terrorist network and its evil allies.

Wherever found, all human suffering needs the healing Gospel of Christ. Our churches need to reach out to Africa and the rest of the world. Africa is being "terrorized," this time by AIDS. Each week, over 50,000 African souls die from the disease. Each week, those 50,000 Africans who die are replaced with 70,000 more who are newly affected with HIV.[96] The disease's consequences are grim and disturbing. Besides Africa, the pandemic affects large numbers of people in Southeast Asia, South America, the Caribbean, and Eastern Europe.[97] According to estimates, over 70 million deaths from AIDS will occur by 2020 in the most affected 45 countries.[98]

Consequences are also grim in the U.S. Most Americans do not realize that the face of AIDS has changed in the U.S. from what it was in the late '70s and early '80s. AIDS is the leading cause of death among African Americans ages 25-44. Sexual exploitation of adolescent girls by older men and sexual irresponsibility among teens in general have contributed to changing the typical population group with AIDS, or who are at risk to contract the disease. Complicating the matter, sexual myths and dishonesty abound. Far too often, men believe that having sex with virgins will prevent AIDS. Similarly, sexual partners fail to disclose their HIV status, and bisexuality (particularly among the Black male prison-released population) often remains hidden from sexual partners. AIDS is an epidemic among the poor and people of color, and its numbers are spreading rapidly among females.[99]

Considering the wealth and prosperity in the U.S., it is a shameless scourge that in the South there are some AIDS/HIV populations and conditions that are on a par with Africa and other "two-thirds" world populations. In the South a doubling of actual AIDS cases has occurred in seven years. This is true for instance, of places in Mississippi and Alabama. Southern rural areas are experiencing an AIDS epidemic.

A gospelizing forerunner of ministry to AIDS victims in the South is the Rev. Dr. Ronald Myers, M.D. In the history of Black churches in America, Dr. Myers is the first ordained and commissioned medical missionary to the Mississippi Delta, the nation's poorest region. He has served the area since 1988, and maintains his Mississippi practice in Tchula (Holmes County), and Belzoni (Humphreys County). Dr. Myers states:

"These areas of Mississippi are the two-thirds world in the U.S. The destitute environment and severe conditions of AIDS, sexually transmitted diseases, and other factors affecting the health and lives of infants give a child born in Bangladesh a better chance of survival than a child born in the Mississippi Delta."[100]

An article entitled "On the Road in Third World Alabama," graphically details the socio-economic conditions in Alabama's Choctaw County. Extended families inhabit rusted out trailer homes, without electricity, running water, and indoor plumbing. Their income is poverty level, and there are multiple teen pregnancies. They have no medical insurance, and they experience the insensitive politics and bureaucracy of acquiring scant medicine and medical care. There are no hospitals or infectious disease doctors in Choctaw County. AIDS/HIV infection, disease complications such as pneumonia, myths and denial about AIDS (often kept secret by those who are suffering), infected "sexual networks," refusing to be tested, family and community abandonment, Church rejection, isolation, depression, lingering illness, horror, hopelessness, and death—these are the conditions we would expect to have reported in the news about other poor people, other impoverished countries, other destitute lands. Sadly, the wasting devastation exists right here in U.S., at the back doors of our wealth and inhumane neglect.[101]

Though the AIDS/HIV pandemic and epidemics are but one of a myriad of terrorizing problems facing humanity, its magnitude demands very serious attention, especially by the people of God. To repeat, AIDS is a poor peoples' disease, and the poor are the heart of Jesus' gospelizing. There were fewer than 3,000 deaths associated with the attack of September 11, 2001. AIDS deaths are well over 50,000 each week worldwide.[102] These astounding numbers of deaths the world over continue to rise. Like a raging forest fire, AIDS has not been contained.

The U.S. government and its people graciously responded to the terror of September 11 by allocating tens of billions of dollars. By comparison, the financial response to the AIDS terror-epidemic *in the U.S.* has been pathetic, not to mention the response to the AIDS pandemic in Africa and other places.[103]

Many other world populations are victims of terror and the evils of inhumanity to humankind. Reference can be made to continued fratricide and genocide by African peoples and "ethnic cleansing" in Eastern Europe. Forms of human slavery are yet practiced in some Islamic nations. Pakistan and India approach the precipice of nuclear war. The Palestinian-Israel geo-political, religious hotbed over homeland territory continues to disrupt the potential for peace with cycles of racial-religious hatred, oppression, terror, forced occupation, terror, suicide bombings, terror. Entrenched inter-cultural tensions and warfare are causing refugee camps and forced migration to flourish. There is the economic-survival terrorism of sweatshops and child labor in Mexico, India, Thailand, and other countries. Women are being forced into sterilization in China. There is the genital circumcision, i.e., mutilation, and forced prostitution of young African girls and others. Due to a lack of options, Eastern European women are compelled into sexual slavery in Kosovo. In the U.S. a growing gap in income continues between the rich and the poor; there is a growing housing shortage, especially for the poor; there is a skyrocketing growth in uninsured people, seriously affecting health care and the general quality of life.

Humanity is in a season and moment of terror; there is terror in Africa and other continents, terror among nations and groups, world terror, and personal terror. However, the world's worst moment is the Church's greatest challenge.

Intimidating moments and seasons of terrorism have created for the Church a great responsibility and opportunity.[104]

As followers of Christ, we should seize this chance to proclaim and bring the message of God's eternal Good News to a lost and hurting humanity. A change is divinely demanded of us.

Though we ourselves are already victims of terror, **as believers in Christ, we must nevertheless *gospelize*.** Despite personal issues and pressures, we can't wait for better and more conducive times; we ought not place on hold the gospelizing work of Christ. These "distressing times"[105] demand of churches and individuals a radical reordering of Christian priorities and ministry. They require an unprecedented outward-movement, advancing God's eternal kingdom and redeeming Gospel in our world. In the midst of remembering and reconciliation, revenge and retaliation, repenting and restitution, there is no substitute for **rising up and reaching out** with the Gospel.

Christians must think and operate differently. We must change, now. Christ's love for humanity and His gospelizing mission—coupled with the critical needs of people—inescapably compels Christ's Gospelizers to act. All churches must (re)structure their practices and programs. Using all our available energies and resources, our churches must go out and bring forth to the people the Gospel message and ministry of Christ's redeeming work. In the open and wasting spaces we must *herald* and *manifest* the Resurrection presence of Christ—holistically manifest the Good News of His presence and redemption—face-to-face with an increasingly devastated world community.

Urgently, all believers and churches must gospelize the multitudes who are increasingly burdened with intimidating fears, unnerving vulnerability, widespread hopelessness, deep-seated anger and resentment, uncertain tomorrows, and survival-threatening hours and occurrences. Here is our chance—and it could very well be our final season of opportunity before Christ returns[106]—here is our chance to bring the Good News of Christ and the blessings of His eternal salvation to humanity's heavy-laden. The LORD's prophetic voice is calling the Church in America — calling our own "terrorized" communities of believers — to become Gospelizers.

My hope is that the Church's spirit of *gospelizing* will intensify and surpass the spirit of terror that has gripped our world since September 2001.

It has in my own life.

8

A Gospelizing Theology

Essential Biblical Data and Observations

for Developing

A Theology-Missiology of Gospelizing/Gospelizers

As a Biblical word exposition and study *Gospelizers!* explicates and promotes a theological perspective. In this chapter I will summarize Biblical data and principles that are essential for developing a theology of gospelizing and Gospelizers. The particular dimension of theology being informed is missiology, the character and purpose of the witness and mission of believers and the Church. Some of this information was introduced in previous chapters.

The word being studied is the verb *euangelizo* (*euangelizomai*), and is translated "gospelizing." The Biblical data for *euangelizo* is predominantly found in the writings of Luke, the beloved physician, historian, and theologian. Luke's Gospel and Acts (Luke's two-part treatise) uses *euangelizo* 25 times: ten times in the former book, and fifteen times in the latter. His use totals almost half the term's 54 occurrences appearing in New Testament writings. Additionally, Paul uses the term 21 times, the Hebrews writer two times, Peter three times (in his first epistle), and John two times (in the Revelation).

Gospelizing Connects
the Gospel of Luke to Acts and
the Ministry of Jesus to the Ministry of the Church

Luke--------------*euangelizo*-----------The Acts
Jesus' Ministry------*gospelizing*------Church Ministry

Luke's use of *euangelizo* is particularly interesting—unique among the other Gospel writers. Only Matthew uses the term, and that occurs a single time. In Luke's Gospel we often find the term coming from the lips of Jesus. In complementary fashion, we also find the term being used of the *euangelizo* activity in the early Church. Thus, there is a pertinent connection between the *euangelizo* ministry of Christ and of Christ's Church. As co-workers with Her Lord, the Church continues the *euangelizo* ministry begun by Christ in His earthly sojourn.

Euangelizo is used intensively in several ways in a few passages. We have already noted its usage in Luke's writings (25 times in Luke—Acts). In Acts 8 *euangelizo* is used five times: verses 4, 12, 25, 35, and 40. In Galatians 1, the term is used six times: verses 1, 8 (twice), 9, 11, 16, and 23. First Corinthians 9:15-18 uses the term three times: verses 16 (twice), and 18. *Euangelizo* is used alongside the noun *euangelion* (Gospel) in four passages: 1 Corinthians 15:1; 2 Corinthians 11:7; Galatians 1:11; and Revelation 14:6. Finally, the term is used alongside the adjective *agathos* in Romans 10:15. I have limited this chapter to a summary of those occurrences. They reveal a dimension of intensive use of one sort or another, and the Biblical student should note their emphasis when forming a theology.

The Gospel of Luke

In reference to Christ, *euangelizo* appears in Luke 2:10; 4:18; 4:43; 7:22; 8:1; 9:6; 16:16; and 20:1. Following are insights gained from this usage.

Luke 2:8-20 is the gospelizing announcement of the Savior's birth by angels to shepherds. Luke 2:10 reads: "But the angel said to them, 'Do not be afraid; for see—I am bringing you good news *[gospelizing]* of great joy for all the people.'"

Observations:
- An angel gospelized the coming/birth of the Savior, who is Christ the Lord.
- Shepherds, a poor and lowly class, received the gospelizing announcement.
- The sign of the gospelizing revealed a lowly Savior, wrapped in bands of cloth, lying in a manger.
- The response of heaven to the gospelizing announcement was the worship of God in the highest heaven.
- The overall effect of gospelizing the Savior Christ was that the Lord brings "Peace" to humanity (cf. Acts 10:36).

Luke 4:16-22 is the record of Jesus gospelizing the Jubilee. Luke 4:18-19 reads: "[18] The Spirit of the Lord is upon me, because he has anointed me to bring good news *[gospelize]* to the poor. He has sent me to proclaim release to the captives and recovery of sight to the blind, to let the oppressed go free, [19] to proclaim the year of the Lord's favor."

Observations:
- Jesus gospelizes the Jubilee to humanity as the fulfillment of His mission.

- The Spirit of the Lord anointed Jesus for gospeliz-
  ing the Jubilee.
- Gospelizing the Jubilee to the poor was the focus
  and thrust of Jesus' ministry.
- Gospelizing the Jubilee to the poor is socially liber-
  ating and empowering.
- Gospelizing the Jubilee is the year of God's favor;
  God's *kairotic* moment (His seasonal opportunity).

**Luke 4:40-44 is a record of Jesus' gospelizing at Caper-
naum.** Luke 4:43 reads: "But he said to them, 'I must
proclaim the good news *[gospelize]* of the kingdom of God
to the other cities also; for I was sent for this purpose.'"

Observations:
- Christ's gospelizing includes healing the sick and
  exorcising demons from those who are possessed.
- Christ gospelized the kingdom of God — God's rule
  in the heart, lives, and affairs of humanity.
- Gospelizing in new places was an imperative for
  Christ.
- Christ was sent on His mission for the purpose of
  gospelizing.

**Luke 7:18-22 is the record of Jesus' gospelizing for John
the Baptist who sought to determine whether Jesus was
"the one to come," or whether the people should wait for
another.** Luke 7:22 reads: "And he [Jesus] answered, 'Go
and tell John what you have seen and heard: the blind receive their sight, the lame walk, the lepers are cleansed, the
deaf hear, the dead are raised, the poor have good news
brought to them *[are gospelized]*.'"

Observations:
- Through His gospelizing, Jesus authenticated Him-
  self as the One who had come.
- Jesus' gospelizing was holistic, including words

and acts of salvation; what was "seen and heard," and a full range of healing cures.

- Jesus authenticated His ministry by gospelizing "the poor." Gospelizing the poor receives greater emphasis than even the dead being raised.
- The person is "blessed" who is not offended by Jesus and His gospelizing.

Luke 8:1-3 is the record of Jesus' second gospelizing campaign. Luke 8:1a reads: "Soon afterwards he [Jesus] went on through cities and villages, proclaiming and bringing the good news [*gospelizing*] of the kingdom of God."

Observations:

- By gospelizing, Jesus proclaimed God's kingdom and manifested a greater and complementary ministry to a herald's announcement.
- Gospelizing was the initiative of Jesus.
- Jesus' gospelizing mission included specially chosen followers, "the Twelve," as well as "unofficial" followers: certain women, and many others. They were a community of gospelizers.
- Gospelizers who accompanied Jesus had been healed spiritually and physically of evil spirits and sicknesses.
- Financially capable women supported Jesus' gospelizing mission.

Luke 9:1-6 is the record of the gospelizing mission of the Twelve. Luke 9:6 reads: "They departed and went through the villages, bringing the good news [*gospelizing*] and curing diseases everywhere."

Observations:

- Jesus commissioned the Twelve to gospelize the kingdom of God.

- Jesus gave them gospelizing power over demons and authority and to cure diseases.
- Jesus instructed them when gospelizing to trust God's provision for their needs, identify with the people they gospelized, and adjust to rejection of their gospelizing.
- Sent by Jesus, the "Twelve" fulfilled their gospelizing commission.

Luke 16:14-18 records Jesus' rejoinder to the ridiculing Pharisees. Luke 16:16 reads: "The law and the prophets were in effect until John came; since then the good news of the kingdom of God is proclaimed [*gospelized*]."

Observations:
- Gospelizing transcends/replaces the law and prophets' tradition of the Old Covenant faith community.
- Gospelizing opposes all materialistic human values and value-systems.[107]
- The effectualness of gospelizing causes a "forced" entry into the kingdom of God.

Luke 20:1-8 records a challenge to Christ's authority to gospelize, and His response to the challengers. Luke 20:1 reads: "One day, as he [Jesus] was teaching the people in the temple and telling the good news [*gospelizing*], the chief priests and the scribes came with the elders."

Observations:
- Jesus gospelized in the temple, teaching and "doing things," and healing (cf. Matthew 21:14).
- The Jewish religious leadership challenged the authority of Jesus to gospelize.
- Jesus established that His authority to gospelize came from God in heaven; it did not originate from human sources.

- Jesus defended His authority to gospelize, and challenged the ungodly system of the temple's religious leaders.

The Acts

The Acts (of Jesus through the Holy Spirit in the Church) complements the use of *euangelizo* in Luke's Gospel. In reference to Christ, *euangelizo* appears in Acts 5:42; 8:4, 12, 25, 35, 40; 10:36; 11:20; 13:32; 14:7, 15, 21; 15:35; 16:10; and 17:18. The following insights highlight the first seven occurrences. They take us from the first persecution against the Church (5:42), to the conversion of the Gentile Cornelius (10:36).

Acts 5:12-42 is the first record of the persecution against the gospelizing Church, and how the believers responded. Acts 5:42 reads: "And every day in the temple and at home they did not cease to teach and proclaim *[gospelize]* Jesus as the Messiah."

Observations:
- The apostles' gospelizing gave rise to the persecution. They did "signs and wonders," and "cures." Many "believers were added to the Lord," and "they were all together," in the *Koinonia*, the Church community. Others came to Jerusalem to experience the gospelizing (5:12-16).
- Jewish religious authorities resisted the gospelizing by arresting, imprisoning, and ordering the apostles to cease speaking in Jesus' name. But the Lord miraculously released them from prison and commanded them to "Go, stand in the temple and tell the people the whole message about this life" (5:20). The apostles obeyed and "went on with their teaching" in the temple (5:21-25).
- The Jewish religious authorities re-arrested the

apostles and reprimanded them for rejecting orders "not to teach in this name" (5:28). But the apostles defended their position to gospelize by saying, "We must obey God rather than any human authority," and proceeded to gospelize the religious leaders (5:29-32).

- The religious leaders "were enraged and wanted to kill" the apostles (5:33). Gamaliel advised and warned them to back away from their murderous intent. If the apostles' gospelizing was a plan and undertaking of God, it could not be overthrown, and opposition to it would be opposition against God (5:35-39a).
- The religious leaders heeded Gamaliel's counsel and released the apostles, but not before flogging and ordering them "not to speak in the name of Jesus," i.e., not to gospelize (5:40).
- The apostles responded by rejoicing for being persecuted "for the sake of the name" (5:41). In obedience to God and defiance of human authority, "…every day in the temple and at home they did not cease to teach and proclaim *[gospelize]* Jesus as the Messiah" (5:42).

Acts 8:1-4 is the record of a severe persecution against the Church and their gospelizing in response. Acts 8:4 reads: "Now those who were scattered went from place to place, proclaiming *[gospelizing]* the word."

Observations:
- The death of Stephen sparked Saul's severe persecution that scattered the church in Jerusalem throughout Judea and Samaria.
- As the church scattered they decentralized to gospelize the word.
- The whole Church, both men and women, became Gospelizers.

Acts 8:5-13 is the record of Philip's gospelizing in Samaria. Acts 8:12 reads: "But when they believed Philip, who was proclaiming the good news [*gospelizing*] about the kingdom of God and the name of Jesus Christ, they were baptized, both men and women."

Observations:
- Philip gospelized across ethnic and cultural lines in Samaria.
- Philip's gospelizing included "proclaiming the Messiah," performing signs, cures, and great miracles.
- Gospelizing was more powerful than the sorceries of Simon who was amazed by Philip's ministry.
- Gospelizing brought joy to the Samaritans, who believed and were baptized, *Koinonia*-ized in response to the message.

Acts 8:14-25 records Peter's and John's gospelizing to the Samaritans, and the exposure and rebuke of Simon the Sorcerer for his materialism and spiritual decadence. Acts 8:25 reads: "Now after Peter and John had testified and spoken the word of the Lord, they returned to Jerusalem, proclaiming the good news [*gospelizing*] to many villages of the Samaritans."

Observations:
- The gospelizing impartation of Peter and John bestowed the Holy Spirit upon the Samaritans, affirming their conversion to Christ and inclusion in His Church.
- Simon the Sorcerer, who sought to purchase the apostles' gospelizing power, exposed his materialism, wicked heart, and condemnation, and cast a shadow over the genuineness of his conversion.
- On their return to Jerusalem, Peter and John gospelized to many villages of the Samaritans.

Acts 8:26-39 records Philip's gospelizing to the Ethiopian Official. Acts 8:35 reads: "Then Philip began to speak, and starting with this scripture, he proclaimed *[gospelized]* to him [the Ethiopian official] the good news about Jesus."

Observations:

- An "angel of the Lord," "the Spirit," sent Philip to gospelize to the Ethiopian official (8:26, 29).
- Philip began gospelizing about Jesus by explaining Isaiah 53:7-8.
- Philip's gospelizing included the Ethiopian's baptism, *Koinonia-izing.*
- Once gospelized, the Ethiopian "went on his way rejoicing" (8:39).

Acts 8:40 records Philip's gospelizing from Azotus to Caesarea. Acts 8:40 reads: "But Philip found himself at Azotus, and as he was passing through the region, he proclaimed *[gospelized]* the good news to all the towns until he came to Caesarea."

Observations:

- The Spirit of the Lord concluded Philip's gospelizing by snatching him away from the Ethiopian official.
- As a matter of course, Philip gospelized to the towns on the way from Azotus to Caesarea.

Acts 10:34-48 records Peter's gospelizing to the household of Cornelius, a Gentile. Acts 10:36 reads: "You know the message he [God] sent to the people of Israel, preaching *[gospelizing]* peace by Jesus Christ—he is Lord of all."

Observations:

- The Jew/Gentile context reveals that God directs and leads in gospelizing across ethno-cultural groups.

- God Himself was gospelizing peace through the coming and life of Jesus, a summation of Christ's work.
- Confessing the Lordship of Jesus Christ is joined with gospelizing peace.
- The gift of the Spirit and water baptism (*Koinonia*-izing) completed the gospelizing by Jews to the Gentiles. Hence, through gospelizing the Church becomes a reconciled community, the *Koinonia*.

Gospelizing Peace

The Luke—Acts exposition of *euangelizo* presented above begins with the announcement of the Savior's birth, and culminates in the conversion of the Gentiles. The theological theme of the gospelizing announcement was "peace" (Luke 2:14). Peter also announced that God sent His message gospelizing "peace" by Jesus Christ to the Gentiles (Acts 10:36). The Apostle Paul noted this same effect of Christ's coming: "So he [Jesus] came and proclaimed *[gospelized]* peace..." (Ephesians 2:17).

Authentic gospelizing brings holistic peace to humanity. It brings sinners who are made righteous into reconciliation with God. It brings a personal internal reconciliation of harmony, rest, calm, and contentment into the inner being of those who trust God's grace. It effects the reconciliation of righteousness between hostile and estranged persons and groups who abide by the Gospel of Christ and His Church. Gospelizing brings the peace of Christ to humanity.

Intensive Use of *Euangelizo* in
Acts 8, Galatians 1, and 1 Corinthians 9

We identify three passages where there is a multiple use of *euangelizo*. The first is **Acts 8**, where the term appears in verses 4, 12, 25, 35, and 40. Specific observations on these verses were covered above. The persecution (ter-rorizing) of the Church is the overriding context of Acts 8, and impacts our understanding and application of gos-pelizing.

The key point is that the terrorized Church decentral-ized and intensified their gospelizing, even cross-culturally. Consequently, they fulfilled the prophetic-imperative words of Jesus: "But you will receive power when the Holy Spirit has come upon you; and you will be my witnesses in Jerusalem, in all Judea and Samaria, and to the ends of the earth" (Acts 1:8). The "ends of the earth" for the early Church was Cush (Biblical Ethiopia). Thus, Christ's words were fulfilled when His messenger Philip ("the evangelist" or gospelizer, Acts 21:8) gospelized the Ethiopian Eunuch. God turned terrorism against the Church into a testimony of the Gospel unto the ends of the earth.[108]

Galatians chapter 1 contains an intensive use of *euan-gelizo*, appearing in verses 1, 8 (twice), 9, 11, 16, and 23. There are several general observations we can make about this letter Paul wrote to the church in Galatia. The book is one of Paul's earliest, systematically theological, and con-tentious epistles (contrast the spirit of Romans). Against the backdrop of Judaizers, Galatians presents and contends for "the truth of the gospel" (2:5, 14).

To gain salvation and spirituality, the Judaizers (Jewish Christians with their non-Jewish converts) sought to exalt the Jewish law and works over the Gospel's grace and faith. Their teaching perverted the Gospel (1:7), disrupted the Church's fellowship (5:7ff.), and restrained the be-liever's freedom in Christ (2:4ff.; 5:1). Their erroneous teaching voided Christ's redeeming work on the cross (2:21; 6:11ff.). In response, the Apostle Paul wrote this very forceful and militant letter to defend the true Gospel, and to correct the false teaching that had "bewitched" the Church (cf. 3:1).

Paul makes the ministry of gospelizing a key point in his argument for the Gospel. The specific verses follow.

Galatians 1:8: "But even if we or an angel from heaven should proclaim to you a gospel [*gospelize*] contrary to what we proclaimed [*gospelized*] to you, let that one be accursed!"

Observations:
- There is only one authentic Gospel to gospelize.
- Paul (with other messengers of Christ) originally gospelized this Gospel to the Galatians.[109]

Galatians 1:9: "As we have said before, so now I repeat, if anyone proclaims to you a gospel [*gospelizes*] contrary to what you received, let that one be accursed!"

Observation:
- Anyone gospelizing a message that differs from the original, authentic Gospel is cursed.

Galatians 1:11: "For I want you to know, brothers and sisters, that the gospel that was proclaimed [*gospelized*] by me is not of human origin."

Observation:
- The Gospel gospelized by the Apostle Paul was a divine message, revelational truth; it did not originate from human reasoning.

Galatians 1:15-16 "[15] But when God, who had set me apart before I was born and called me through his grace, was pleased [16] to reveal his Son to me, so that I might proclaim [*gospelize*] him among the Gentiles, I did not confer with any human being."

Observation:
- God's Son was revealed to Paul so that Paul could gospelize Him to the Gentiles.

Galatians 1:23 "...'The one who formerly was persecuting us is now proclaiming [gospelizing] the faith he once tried to destroy.'"

Observation:
- Paul's gospelizing completely reversed his persecution (terrorization) of the Church.

Based on the above observations, it is imperative that Gospelizers adhere to a Biblical understanding of the Gospel, and stand prepared to defend and propagate "the truth of the Gospel" at all costs. Genuine gospelizing upholds faith, grace, redemption, and freedom in Christ through His atoning death on the cross.

In **1 Corinthians 9** Paul uses *euangelizo* three times: verses 16 (twice), and 18. The context of these verses (15-18) explains how and why the Apostle Paul yielded his rights when gospelizing. By applying principles of Christian freedom and responsibility, Paul yielded his rights by foregoing financial support from the Corinthians whom he gospelized.

1 Corinthians 9:16: "If I proclaim the gospel [gospelize], this gives me no ground for boasting, for an obligation is laid on me, and woe to me if I do not proclaim the gospel [gospelize]!"

Observations:
- Gospelizing was Paul's duty; doing it was not his privilege to choose.
- Paul understood the adverse consequences he would incur for not gospelizing.

1 Corinthians 9:18: "What then is my reward? Just this: that in my proclamation *[gospelizing]* I may make the gospel free of charge, so as not to make full use of my rights in the gospel."

Observation:
- Paul chose to gospelize the Corinthians without obligating them for financial support.

Based on these verses, the message conveyed is that Gospelizers must promote and protect their gospelizing among unbelievers/new converts. Gospelizers must never become materialistic, and must never allow financial roadblocks to hinder the Gospel's effects. When gospelizing, Gospelizers must be prepared to yield their rights (cf. 1 Corinthians 9:19-23).

Gospelizing and the Gospel

Four passages are special, for in them *euangelizo* is used alongside the noun *euangelion* (Gospel): 1 Corinthians 15:1; 2 Corinthians 11:7; Galatians 1:11; and Revelation 14:6.

1 Corinthians 15:1: "Now I would remind you, brothers and sisters, of the good news that I proclaimed to you *[of the Gospel that I gospelized to you]*, which you in turn received, in which also you stand."

2 Corinthians 11:7: "Did I commit a sin by humbling myself so that you might be exalted, because I proclaimed God's good news *[I gospelized God's Gospel]* to you free of charge?"

Galatians 1:11: "For I want you to know, brothers and sisters, that the gospel that was proclaimed *[the gospel gospelized]* by me is not of human origin."

Revelation 14:6: "Then I saw another angel flying in mid-heaven, with an eternal gospel to proclaim *[Gospel to gospelize]* to those who live on the earth—to every nation and tribe and language and people."

Observations:

- These four passages intensify the Gospel message being conveyed. They stress the specific content of gospelizing: the Gospel revelation. Once introduced to the public, certain ideas and words often attain a different meaning than originally intended. The Gospel should always define the meaning of gospelizing.
- Gospelizing the Gospel is the message and work of the Church. We do not gospelize our nation, our personal philosophies, our political ideologies, our material prosperity, or the like. We gospelize the authentic and original Gospel of Jesus Christ and the early Church. The Gospel is always contextualized, socially and culturally. But the context of gospelizing must never overshadow, enslave, or neutralize the Gospel message.

Gospelizing and Good

Romans 10:15, a Scripture that is most precious to preachers and lovers of the Gospel, intensifies the concept of the "good" in gospelizing. *Euangelizo* ("to bring good news") is used alongside the adjective *agathos* ("good"). Its context is Romans 10:14-17, in which the Apostle Paul is explaining the process of gospelizing to bring salvation.

Romans 10:15: "And how are they to proclaim *[kerusso]* him unless they are sent? As it is written, 'How beautiful are the feet of those who bring good news! *[Gospelizers!]*'"

Textual Considerations:

- The KJV reads: "And how shall they preach, ex-

cept they be sent? as it is written, How beautiful
are the feet of them that preach the gospel of peace,
and bring glad tidings of good things!"

- The KJV phrase, "them that preach the gospel of
  peace" is inserted from the Greek translation of the
  Hebrew Old Testament (the Septuagint).[110]
- The KJV phrase "bring glad tidings of good
  things!" is very literal and preferable, whereas the
  NRSV truncates "good things" (*agathos*).
- The sentence is better translated: "How beautiful
  are the feet of **Gospelizers of good things**" (emphasis mine).

Observations:

- Gospelizers bring a good message to their hearers;
  genuine gospelizing is always good for faith-
  obedient hearers of the word.
- The collective witness of Gospelizers gives strength
  to their gospelizing.
- The coming of Gospelizers with the goodness of
  their gospelizing is timely, beautiful, and graceful
  to a lost humanity and a bad news world.

Missiological Clarity Yields Gospelizing Intensity

I encourage those who are so inclined to develop their
theological understanding of Gospelizers and gospelizing,
using these passages and others to form the basic content
of their message. A theology-missiology of gospelizing/
Gospelizers should significantly intersect with and impact
the other branches of Christian theology. Clarity of missiology facilitates gospelizing focus and intensity. A correct
understanding and genuine appreciation of this Biblical
data ought to motivate believers to fulfill our redemptive
mission with Christ. It will "convince, rebuke, and encourage" the Church as we "proclaim the message" and
"do the work of [a Gospelizer]" (cf. 2 Timothy 4:2, 5).

Part III:

Development and Destination

Gospelize to *Koinonia*-ize.

In Part One, we presented the impetus and imperative of Gospelizers, and then we explained the identity and paradigm of Gospelizers — who emerged with intensity in a terrorizing social context and resistance — in Part Two. Now we can cover the third connecting link in this work: the development and destination of gospelizing ministry. So, there was first an urgent motivation, second the holistic models, and third the continuing ministry.

Part III focuses on the third challenge to our churches, to institute a Gospelizers' teaching-discipleship ministry. The Church must develop Gospelizers and their gospelizing to achieve effectiveness in this ministry, which should have several specific aims. The following chapters explore these aims.

The basic aim of a teaching-discipleship ministry is to transform all Christ's disciples into Gospelizers. As they mature and become able, these Gospelizers should be commissioned to the harvest-fields of humanity. In the harvest-fields they will do ministry—holistic ministry in Christ's Name—meeting essential and critical human needs especially among and on behalf of the least/poor of our societies. Ultimately, through their holistic ministry Gospelizers will bring the Church—the *Koinonia*, Community of Christ—to the harvest-fields. Christ's presence in His Community (the Church) will be organized to serve the ongoing needs of converts. Also, the gospelizing churches will challenge the ungodly and inhumane systems of the world that exacerbate human evil and suffering in opposition to Christ's kingdom of God that believers gospelize. As these churches mature they will commission their own Gospelizers who will replicate the process, and thus multiply the churches. This is the destination.

Achieving this goal requires two changes. One, our churches should be (re)structured for accomplishing a gospelizing mission-purpose, and around the kind of teaching-discipleship ministry that will effectively develop Gospelizers. Two, concentrating on gospelizing demands a maximization of believers' resources: time, season, program, human, financial, and property. The Church must reprioritize the allocation of its resources in order to maximize the Gospelizers' ministry.

The Church's Mission-Purpose

The **mission-purpose** of the Church is to *gospelize* in the Name of Christ with a view toward organizing other churches—insuring in the process that the trust of the Gospel is committed, preserved, and transmitted personally, ethno-culturally, and globally from one generation of Christ's disciples to the next.

9

Transforming Disciples
into Gospelizers

The Call:
•Institute a *Gospelizers'* teaching-discipleship ministry.

The teaching-discipleship ministry of *Gospelizers* in the Church is three-fold and involves transforming disciples, commissioning them to the harvest-fields, and multiplying their population into additional churches of like nature.

The Church is called to "make disciples" for Christ. Once these disciples are transformed into *Gospelizers,* the Lord will use them to fulfill the Church's mission-purpose. In this vein we will consider five points: *the Master, the mandate, the mission, the ministry,* and *the movement.*

Overview

Jesus the **Master** charged His followers to "make disciples of all nations" (Matthew 28:19). This resurrection command of Jesus is the **mandate** for His Church throughout the world, and for every generation of believers until the Lord returns. The mandate of Jesus translates into the **mission** of the Church; the Church ascribes to no other purpose. In order to remain true to Christ and maintain the integrity of His Body, the mission given by Christ for His Church must permeate the overall **ministry** of each and every local congregation. Thus, the program of our individual congregations ought to embody the mission of the Church as a whole. In doing so, the **movement** of gospelizing takes place and the Church fulfills its mission-purpose.[111]

The Master—Jesus Christ the Lord

The Scripture reveals to us the Word of God. This Word has come to us through the Lord Jesus Christ, our Savior. Jesus is the great Head of the Church, which is His Body. He has purchased the Church with His own atoning blood. "Keep watch over yourselves and over all the flock, of which the Holy Spirit has made you overseers, to shepherd the church of God that he obtained with the blood of his own Son" (Acts 20:28).

As the Head of the Church, Christ is with His Church all the time. He is the source of the Church's life, and the One Who holds together the Body. Jesus said, "...where two or three are gathered together in my name, there I am in the midst of them" (Matthew 18:20). Jesus is Lord of the Church. He said, "All authority in heaven and in earth has been given to me" (Matthew 28:18). Finally Jesus said, **"I am with you always..."** (Matthew 28:20b, emphasis mine).

The Master Gave the Mandate

As Lord of the Church, the **Master** has commanded His Body. Following Jesus' resurrection, and prior to His ascension back to heaven, the Lord gave a most authoritative command to His disciples. He gave a word from God deserving to be heard by all. Jesus our LORD set the pattern and gave the mandate. This Biblical mandate, recorded in Matthew 28:18-20, is known as Christ's "Great Commission."

> 18 And Jesus came and said to them, "All authority in heaven and on earth has been given to me. 19 Go therefore and **make disciples of all nations,** baptizing them in the name of the Father and of the Son and of the Holy Spirit, 20 and teaching them to obey everything that I have commanded you. And remember, I am with you always, to the end of the age" (emphasis mine).

Understanding the Mandate to Make Disciples

The resurrected Lord, Jesus Christ, has given to us His disciples, His great commission. This command is for us to "teach all nations" (KJV). Modern translations add clarity to these words. The command given by Christ is for His Church to *"make disciples of all nations."* This mandate is Christ's absolute command—His final charge given to His disciples before He left earth and ascended to heaven, fully expecting its fulfillment prior to His return from glory. This is the great commission of Christ. Jesus said, "Go therefore and make disciples of all nations" (Matthew 28:19a).

Our understanding of Who the Church is and Her mission in the world comes from the Word of God. The Holy Spirit of God illumines God's Word, and empowers believers for their work. The Holy Spirit graces us with spiritual gifts for strength and service. Once saved, the followers of Jesus—through faith, grace, teaching, and personal discipline—become saints, servants, stewards, and soldiers[112] for the Lord. These are disciples of Christ.

The Church of Christ is commanded to make disciples for Jesus Christ among **all nations.**[113] Practically, this means that among every people of the world the Church should be present, teaching and leading Her members into becoming Christ-centered in all areas of life. She leads them into being both the Body of Christ and in doing the work of the Body, the Church. For Christ is the Head of the Church, His Body.[114]

Commission, Preservation, Transmission of the Gospel

The work of making disciples is confirmed by the words of Christ in Matthew 28:20. Jesus said, "...teaching them **to obey everything** that I have commanded you" (v. 20a, emphasis mine). The dimension of "commission" is evident in these words. Disciples are those who "obey everything." They are committed to obedience to the word of Christ. It is ludicrous and hypocritical for Christians to claim the name "disciple" but fail to adhere in commitment to the teachings of their Master.

Here there is also an implicit word of preservation. These words of Jesus speak to the Church in terms of Christ's followers continuing faithfully in the apostles' doctrine, as described in Acts 2:42: "They [the earliest believers] **devoted themselves to the apostles' teaching** and fellowship, to the breaking of bread and the prayers" (emphasis mine). In this summary of the earliest stages of the Church there was already developed and **preserved** what could be called "the apostles' teaching."

Shortly after Pentecost, the instruction given by Christ to His original disciples/apostles was systematized and codified enough as a body of truth to be taught and practiced by those converted through the apostles' witness. The mandate of Christ was preserved in "the apostles' teaching." And being preserved, it was capable of being transmitted to the second generation of believers/disciples, who daily devoted themselves to its practice.

Intergenerational Transmission

The Gospel is a trust. Paul wrote, "but just as we have been approved by God to be **entrusted** with the message of the gospel, even so we speak, not to please mortals, but to please God who tests our hearts." And he wrote of "...the glorious gospel of the blessed God, which he **entrusted** to me" (1 Thessalonians 2:4; 1 Timothy 1:11, emphasis mine).

Inherent in the transmission of the trust of the Gospel is both commission and preservation. Those who are faithful to their commitment maintain their trust in the Gospel. These faithful persons must see to it that they preserve the Gospel unstained, that they in turn might deliver it to the generation of believers/disciples succeeding them.[115]

The words of Jesus in Matthew 28:20 provide a connection between Christ and successive Christian generations: **"teaching them to obey everything that I have commanded you"** (emphasis mine). Here the link is between Christ, His original disciples/apostles, and others who would follow Christ based on the witness and teaching of those disciples/apostles. In other words, Jesus commanded His disciples, "You teach them—those who believe in Me through your witness—to be obedient to what I have commanded you."

The Apostle Paul followed this intergenerational pattern of making disciples and transmitting God's word through Jesus. Paul wrote these words to Timothy: "You then, my child, be strong in the grace that is in Christ Jesus; and **what you have heard from me through many witnesses entrust to faithful people who will be able to teach others as well**" (2 Timothy 2:1-2, emphasis mine). Clearly this message refers to four generations of believers: the Apostle Paul, Timothy (Paul's "child"), "faithful people," and "others." Paul conveyed the same idea of transmission to the Corinthian church when he taught them the Gospel: "For I handed on to you as of first importance what I in turn had received" (1 Corinthians 15:3a).

Intergenerational transmission of the Gospel of Christ takes place in four dimensions. First and foremost is **person-to-person.** Nothing substitutes for one disciple of Christ taking the time and energy to make one more disciple for Christ. Second is **ethno-cultural group by ethno-cultural group.** The "nation" contextualization of the Gospel message and the ministry of making disciples are paramount. Effective *gospelizing* never diminishes the racial/ethno-cultural distinctive and context of the hearers and recipients of the Gospel of Christ.[116] Third is the **global** outlook. Intergenerational transmission of the Gospel must reach the entire world. Jesus said, "And this good news of the kingdom will be proclaimed **throughout the world,** as a testimony to all the nations; and then the end will come" (Matthew 24:14, emphasis mine). Jesus also said, "...you will be my witnesses...**to the ends of the earth**" (Acts 1:8, emphasis mine). Finally, there is the **time** dimension. Simply, Jesus said, "And remember, I am with you **always,** to the end of the age" (Matthew 28:20b, emphasis mine). The intergenerational transmission of the Gospel must continue unabated until the end of time, when the Lord returns. And until then, Jesus is with us **"all the days"** (literally).

The Mandate is the Mission

The Church's Reason for Existence

Since the mandate of Jesus is for His Church to "make disciples of all nations," the Church must obey Her Lord by submitting Herself to this purpose. To "make disciples of all nations" is the reason for the existence of the Church in the world. Otherwise, once saved, the Lord would have been pleased to immediately remove the Church from the world! But He hasn't! Therefore, the mandate of the resurrected Lord for the Church is in fact the very mission of the Church. Other than this, the Church needs to search for no other purpose. **The mandate of Christ is the mission of the Church.** It is our mission throughout the world and down through each generation.

The Church's Unique Mission

This mission of "making disciples" for Christ is the unique work of the Church—the Church Who is the Body of Christ in the world. And Jesus—through the grace of His presence, the truth of His Word, and the help of the Holy Spirit—has fully equipped His Church to effectively accomplish this great mission. This mission of Christ has been entrusted to His Church. It has not been entrusted to para-church organizations, or to "ministries" that do not function in the nature of a church.

Maintaining the Church's Mission-Focus

Since making disciples is the mission of the Church, the Church is consequently obligated to maintain this mission-focus in all Her endeavors. Basically, this means that Jesus' disciples should 1) win the lost to Christ and His salvation, and 2) lead believers among all people to become faithful followers of the Lord. This motivation and focus should always remain at the center of whatever good works our churches perform. And this goal should compel the Church throughout this world, and in each generation.

Making Disciples For Christ

The Church is called to "make disciples," but not to make disciples *for us*. Neither the Body of Christ (the Church), nor Her leaders, nor Her members, are called to make disciples for us ourselves. The command is for us to make disciples **for the Lord Jesus Christ,** our Savior. This distinction is subtle, but oh, so necessary!

Unmistakably, *the mission of the Church* — of all of us together and of each of us personally — *is to make disciples for
Jesus.* It is Christ Whom we see, Who gives us power, to
Whom we pledge our wholehearted commitment, after
Whom we pattern our entire way of thinking and living,
and to Whom ultimately we must give account of ourselves. In the highest sense, believers are essentially
disciples of Christ alone, and of no one, or of nothing else.

The Mission Dictates the Ministry

Since the mission of the Church is to "make disciples"
of all nations, how, we may ask, does the Church fulfill
this mission in a manifested ministry? How does the mission of the Church come to permeate the overall ministry
of each local congregation?

A three-phase process gives the answer. The ministry
of the Church makes disciples for Jesus Christ by *gospelizing the lost, receiving converts,* and *sanctifying those
received.*

Gospelizing to Win Conversions to Christ

The primary ministry of the Church is to win conversions to Christ and to His Church through *gospelizing.*
Gospelizers give a holistic witness and mission for Christ
by their gospelizing. The driving force of gospelizing is
the desire to win the lost. The center of our motivation is
to save some sinner, to bring some wanderer home to
God's fold. Nothing can substitute for gospelizing the
Gospel of Jesus Christ. The Lord has chosen "through the
foolishness of our proclamation *[kerygma]*, to save those
who believe" (1 Corinthians 1:21b). But "How are they
[lost souls] to hear without someone to proclaim
[kerusso][117] him?" (Romans 10:14b). They can't. By our
gospelizing the Gospel of Christ — by proclaiming, performing, and imparting Christ's death, burial, resurrection,

and appearances, and free gift of salvation by grace through repentance and faith in His Name—the Church wins conversions. The lost are converted to Christ through the Gospel of God's grace. And their conversion is authentic and holistic.

Gospelizing effects a conversion to Christ that is genuine and whole. The Gospel makes its salvation appeal to each individual as a whole person living in a social and cultural context, and elicits a trust response to the grace and call of the Lord Jesus Christ that impacts the convert in the whole of life. Genuine gospelizing allows no room for a shallow salvation invitation that is tantamount to eliciting a response from a sinner who gives mere mental assent to simplistically understood or uncontextualized Biblical statements, or to sterile theological concepts. The Rev. Clarence L. Hilliard (Chicago) draws attention to a classic model of substantive gospelizing by Paul to the Roman governor Felix:[118]

> 24 Some days later when Felix came with his wife Drusilla, who was Jewish, he sent for Paul and heard him speak concerning faith in Christ Jesus. 25 And as he discussed justice, self-control, and the coming judgment, Felix became frightened and said, "Go away for the present; when I have an opportunity, I will send for you" (Acts 24:24-25).

Paul elicited **"faith in Christ Jesus"** from Felix (and his other hearers) by framing his message in the context of **"justice, self-control, and the coming judgment."** He forcefully called for social responsibility (justice/righteousness) and personal accountability (self-control). The gravity of this contextual invitation to salvation so frightened governor Felix that he became visibly unsettled. The point is clear: gospelizing faith in Christ Jesus requires a sinner to change or to face the prospect of divine judgment for failure to change.

Regeneration is God's gift of grace bestowed on a sinner through an act of wholehearted trust (faith) in Jesus, and is essential salvation and instantaneous. The manifestation of that wholehearted trust is described as "the obedience of faith" (Romans 1:5; 16:26). This "obedience of faith" results in a sinner's repentant break with ungodly thinking and behavior, and shows some significant evidence of a changed life, in both its personal and social dimensions. The convert to Christ responds to the Gospel by submitting to God's will and joining with the Church—Christ's community of fellowship—in a responsible/accountable relationship. The convert also heeds the call of Christ to gospelizing service in the world with Him and His Church. So the convert bears fruit. These are the manifestations of genuine conversion, and the signs of regeneration that are effected by the Gospel.

Genuine gospelizing generates authentic conversions. However, winning conversion to Christ by gospelizing is only the beginning of the process.

Receiving Those Converted into the Church

Another aspect of Church ministry involves receiving those who are converted into the fellowship of a local Christian congregation. Hearing the Gospel not only brings about conversion to Christ, it also brings about inclusion into Christ's community—into His Body, the Church. A sinner's conversion to Christ brings about a "sharing *(koinonia)* in the gospel" (Philippians 1:5; cf. 1:27). *Koinonia* means "fellowship," "communion," "community," "participation," "partnership."[119]

We should not minimize the *"Koinonia-izing"* aspect of conversion. The earliest believers in Christ[120] knew nothing of a concept of personal conversion devoid of public inclusion and commitment to the Church, to the fellowship of the saints. Holistic evangelism includes Church community for converts. For, "day by day the Lord added to their number those who were being saved" (Acts 2:47b).

And those who were saved "devoted themselves to the apostles' teaching and **fellowship**..." (Acts 2:42a, emphasis mine). "And **they were all together** in Solomon's Portico. None of the rest dared **to join them,** but the people held **them** in high esteem. Yet more than ever believers **were added to the Lord,** great numbers of both men and women" (Acts 5:12b-14, emphasis mine).

When a person gets saved, this convert to Christ should be received and "added" — *Koinonia-ized* — into a local fellowship of believers. It is there in the fellowship of the Church that a new believer finds the acceptance and support of the community of faith. Only of the Church did Jesus declare these words: "...upon this rock I will build my church; and the gates of hell shall not prevail against it" (Matthew 16:18b, KJV).

Holistically Sanctifying Those Who are Received

This leads us to a third area of Church ministry. By virtue of the provisions of the Church, new converts to Christ should become holistically sanctified. All believers are to be edified and built up in Christ.

Essentially, through the Church's ministry, new believers should receive grounding in the faith, and embark upon a journey of Christian nurture in both the knowledge and experience of Christ in their lives. If new believers remain faithful, this journey will ultimately lead to full maturity in Christ. They become "spiritual," in contrast to being "natural" (without Christ), "babes" (new believers), or "carnal" (believers controlled by fleshly, worldly, or devilish forces). And their spirituality impacts all of life, and leads to doing social righteousness. Thus, new believers become holistically sanctified. As Paul prayed,

"May the God of peace himself sanctify you entirely; and may your spirit and soul and body be kept sound and blameless at the coming of our Lord Jesus Christ.

The one who calls you is faithful, and he will do this" (1 Thessalonians 5:23-24).

Jesus said to His disciples, "You have already been cleansed by the word I have spoken to you" (John 15:3).

Disciples for Jesus Christ become **learners** of Christ, for a disciple is a "learner," in the sense of a disciplined follower.[121] They become **lovers** of Christ and His followers, for Jesus said, "By this everyone will know that you are my disciples, if you have love for one another" (John 13:35).[122] Ultimately, disciples become **fruit-bearers** in Christ, for Jesus said, "My Father is glorified by this, that you bear much fruit and become my disciples" (John 15:8). So eventually, a holistically sanctified believer will find himself doing the works of Christ, and doing them in fellowship with the Church.

The Ministry Inspires the Movement

Indeed, the fruit-bearing disciples are Gospelizers. When this happens, the disciple-making ministry has become effective. The movement proceeds from learning to doing, from gathering to scattering to spreading the Gospel. The process of the movement is clear.

Initially those who were lost are converted to Christ and received by the Church. The Church works with them to sanctify them in all areas of life. They learn Christ and love Him to the utmost. Their lives are being made whole in the Lord. A transformation is taking place. Becoming transformed, they desire to share the "Good News" that Christ means to them. They are not content just to gather at church. They desire to go forth. So they begin to move out for Christ in response to His gospelizing call. And they move with a living testimony, love, power, and social righteousness. Being spiritually urged to "scatter" into the world, they gospelize wherever they go. They practice the Gospel. They actualize their faith in Christ. Thus, the transformation from disciples to Gospelizers is taking place. The **movement** is on to the harvest-fields. Those who were gospelized become Gospelizers themselves.[123]

Gospelizing by the Whole Church!

Acts 8:1-4 contains a revolutionizing truth: gospelizing is the work of the entire Church. The early believers who were persecuted and scattered included **"both men and women"** (v. 3, emphasis mine, cf. Acts 5:14). And all those who scattered "went from place to place, proclaiming the word" (v. 8:4). Everybody went forth preaching *[gospelizing]* the Gospel; men and women, young and old. All members contributed to the expansion of the Church's witness in their world.[124]

By now, a clear picture should be emerging that all believers in Christ are Gospelizers. All believers are witnesses for Christ on His redeeming mission in the world. The **essential mission of the Church is** *gospelizing,* and *every member of the Church should do gospelizing.* The sole purpose of believers in the world is to become *Gospelizers* for the Lord, both individually and collectively.[125]

10

Commissioning Gospelizers
to the Harvest-Fields

The Call:
•Institute a *Gospelizers'* teaching-discipleship ministry.

The Model of Christ

The second phase of ministry is to commission Gospelizers to the harvest-fields. Once we have transformed disciples into Gospelizers, we then commission these matured followers of Christ. Gospelizers should be equipped for ministry, and then commissioned to do the work of Christ in His Name. In consideration of this we speak of four elements: *the call, the competence, the commissioning, and the covenant.*

Luke 9:1-6
[1] Then Jesus called the twelve together and gave them power and authority over all demons and to cure diseases, [2] and he sent them out to proclaim *[kerusso]*[126] the kingdom of God and to heal. [3] He said to them, "Take nothing for your journey, no staff, nor bag, nor bread,

nor money—not even an extra tunic. 4 Whatever house you enter, stay there, and leave from there. 5 Wherever they do not welcome you, as you are leaving that town shake the dust off your feet as a testimony against them." 6 They departed and went through the villages, bringing the good news *[gospelizing]* and curing diseases everywhere. (Cf. Matthew 10:1-15; Mark 6:7-13)

The Call—*"Jesus called the twelve together"*

A study of the Scripture indicates that this "call" of Jesus to His disciples marked a new phase of His ministry. Earlier the Lord had called these twelve men to become His disciples.[127] Now, as disciples, Jesus calls them together for gospelizing. He commissions them as Gospelizers. There is something formal if not official in this gathering. At this juncture in the work, the call is not randomly geared toward all believers in Christ. This call is made exclusively to "the twelve" whom Jesus made disciples/apostles. They were now transformed enough to become Christ's Gospelizers.

Here is the first step of commissioning modern-day *Gospelizers*. They must be formally called together by the spontaneous and sovereign call of the Spirit of the Lord. And their call must be affirmed through the Lord's Church.[128]

The Competence—*"Jesus...gave them power and authority"*

The competence of the twelve to *gospelize* for Jesus is implied by His giving them "power and authority." Earlier in His ministry Jesus evidently withheld from the twelve this "power and authority," presumably because they had not matured sufficiently (become holistically sanctified), or were not trained enough to do the ministry responsibly. At this point, they were ready. So Jesus "equipped" them for ministry (cf. Ephesians 4:11-12ff.).

Jesus gave "the twelve" the authority and power to do effectual ministry in His "name" (cf. Luke 10:17; Matthew 7:22). This power and authority could be exercised "over all demons and to cure diseases." Here is the impartation dimension of gospelizing. The disciples' ministry produced effectual results. The Scripture says, "On their return the apostles told Jesus all they had done" (Luke 9:10). They cured "diseases everywhere" (Luke 9:6b). The competence of "the twelve" was revealed in the outcomes of their work. As co-workers with the Lord, they worked miracles in Jesus' name.

The Commission—"Jesus...sent them out"

Officially, Jesus commissioned His disciples. The Word tells us "...[Jesus] sent them out to proclaim the kingdom of God and to heal" (Luke 9:2). Mark 6:7 tell us Jesus sent them in pairs, "two by two." Further, "They departed and went through the villages, bringing the good news [gospelizing] and curing diseases everywhere" (Luke 9:6). There was a definite time, place, scope of ministry, and mission-field to which Jesus' disciples were sent. There was a starting point and a culminating point (cf. Luke 9:2, 10). The teaching-discipleship of Jesus was intentional and directional. It led to gospelizing. The twelve were "sent" by Jesus to do His work.

The Church that produces Gospelizers must at some point begin to send them forth, in the name of Christ. This is proactive ministry. This is outreach ministry. This is advancing the Gospel. Sometimes as Christians we fail in our mission because we fail to act with urgency and to formally send out disciples who are prepared and doing the work of gospelizing in the harvest-fields. Let this no longer be our practice. Instead, let us send forth Good News bearers and workers into the Lord's harvest.[129]

The twelve Gospelizers sent forth by Jesus were in covenant with their Lord. Jesus gave them instructions about how to "lead a life worthy of" their calling (cf. Ephesians 4:1). Jesus' "charge" to the twelve is found in Luke 9:3-5 (see also Matthew 10:5-15ff.; Mark 6:8-11).

Jesus expected His disciples to obey His instructions; to stay faithful to the "covenant" He imposed upon them. These instructions imply several things.

The disciples were to trust in the Lord to provide for them and were not to become materialistic ("Take nothing for your journey, no staff, nor bag, nor bread, nor money — not even an extra tunic," Luke 9:3). They were to live among the people they freely served ("Whatever house you enter, stay there, and leave from there," v. 4).[130] They were not to be "handcuffed" by those who did not welcome them or their gospelizing ("Wherever they do not welcome you, as you are leaving that town shake the dust off your feet as a testimony against them," v. 5).

The Harvest-Fields and the Message

The fields for harvesting the mission are the multitudes. The multitudes are the marginalized and victimized of our societies. The Scripture calls them "the lost," "the least/poor," and "the unwell."[131] They are the "afflicted," and the "powerless" of humanity. Often they are downtrodden and rejected, hopeless and despised.

Any person without Christ is "lost." All are candidates for the Gospel. We discussed gospelizing (that is, converting) the lost in chapter 3. Our emphasis here is that Gospelizers must intentionally spread the Gospel and do their righteous works among the poor, the "no-things" of the world (cf. 1 Corinthians 1:26-31). If the Gospel is not Good News for "the poor," then it is not authentically the Gospel of Christ (cf. Luke 7:22-23).

Jesus did His gospelizing among the poor.[132] Sure, He reached others, but His main thrust was with "the least of these" (cf. Matthew 25:40ff.). Jesus ministered to people who were like sheep without a shepherd. He felt compassion for them, for they were harassed and helpless (cf. Mark 6:30-34; Matthew 9:36). Those who were marginalized and victimized could appreciate the fullness of the gospelizing message and ministry: good words, gracious works, and great workings of God. Any church that neglects the poor and the least in our world does not represent Jesus, "the Lord of the harvest" and the Lord of the Church.

Fertile Harvest-Fields

There are fertile harvest-fields in our communities and throughout the world. Several areas of service for *Gospelizers* are very fruitful for ministry.

Gospelizers can Perform a "Gracious Work" — Bringing the "Jubilee Year" to the Least/Poor

Gospelizers can do a most gracious work for the least/poor among us by effecting principles of the Biblical "Jubilee Year." Instituted by the LORD God in the faith-community of the Old Covenant (Leviticus 25:8ff.), the Jubilee Year was brought to supreme fulfillment by Jesus. In Luke 4:18-19, Jesus revealed Himself as the preeminent Gospelizer of the Jubilee Year when He proclaimed,

> **"The Spirit of the Lord is upon me,**
> **because he has anointed me**
> **to bring good news to the poor.**
> **He has sent me to proclaim release to the captives**
> **and recovery of sight to the blind,**
> **to let the oppressed go free,**
> **to proclaim the year of the Lord's favor."**
> (emphasis mine)

The Jubilee originally was designed to break the inter-generational cycle of poverty every 50th year by providing a second chance for the poor of the Hebrew-Israelite nation. It provided for debt-release, land restoration, and re-establishment of family relationships. The poor were granted the opportunity of re-integration into society in a way that was functional and healthy for the whole. On the given day, "Release!" was proclaimed throughout the land. Set free from the captivity of their socio-economic bondage, enslaved persons could reclaim their inheritance and rejoin their families. (See Isaiah 58 and 61 for further insights into the ministry of the Jubilee and the divine demands of effecting its social and systemic righteousness.)

Preached by this author as "The Po' Man's Holiday,"[133] the Jubilee Year was liberating and empowering for the poor—the least important in a society. Poor people—their redemption and welfare—were at the center of the Jubilee, and also at the heart of the LORD, the God Who ordained this radical and revolutionizing celebration.

Empowering the poor of the world is the heart of God. Jesus loved and served the poor. No wonder we find that at the inauguration of His ministry, Jesus established as His "Nazareth Manifesto" the platform of the Jubilee and its complete fulfillment in Himself! Thus, since Jesus so fulfilled the Jubilee, the essence of the celebration's divinely instituted principles and practices are imperative, instructive, and constructive for the Christian community and the societies of our day.

As Gospelizers, we too must love the poor and empower them in God and His world. As Jesus did, so we must gospelize the Jubilee. This is a "gracious work." It is one thing to give the poor a fish. It is another thing to teach the poor how to fish. It is a "Jubilee-thing" to provide the poor with a net, and grant them accessibility to ownership of a pond to develop their own fishing enterprise! Providing the net and the pond is empowerment—it is Jubilee—and it is the ministry of Gospelizers.

Gospelizers can Perform a "Gracious Work" —
Bringing the Homeless into Community

Homelessness has become a scourge in our society. Persons without proper food and shelter are increasing day by day. Not just men. Dispossessed women, families, and children are on the rise. Gospelizers can help arrest the problem and reap the fruit in this harvest-field.

Various strategies can address the issue. Bringing the homeless into **community** will help correct the problem without stripping persons of their dignity, sense of self-worth, and self-determination. The Church of Christ is the new "community." In some way or another, those who are homeless must be brought into a caring and responsible community of Gospelizers. We can protect them, provide for them, and bring them to socio-economic wholeness and interdependence in community. Jesus said, "I was a stranger and you welcomed me" (Matthew 25:35c).

Gospelizers can Impart a "Great Working of God" —
Healing "the Unwell" from HIV/AIDS

Earlier we drew attention to the HIV/AIDS pandemic among African-descended communities and in sub-Saharan Africa. Each week in Africa over 50,000 persons die from AIDS. Further, each week more than 70,000 persons become newly infected with HIV, the virus that precedes AIDS. These catastrophic deaths occur each week in Africa *alone*. To these deaths on the African continent we must add the AIDS-related deaths and HIV infections among persons the world over: in the Caribbean, the U.S., South America, Canada, Eastern Europe, Southeast Asia, China, etc.[134]

In these times, most of the persons dying from AIDS are of African descent. These deaths, with their combined devastation of African populations and societal and ecological environments, are alarming. They are "terrorizing."[135]

In the face of the AIDS/HIV terrorizing pandemic Gospelizers ought to rise to the challenge. We ought to seize the opportunity to impart healing—holistic healing—to those who are "unwell." Gospelizers are "healers," we have "cures."

Holistic Healings of Jesus

Several words are translated "heal" in the Scriptures, including: *therapeuo, iaomai, katharizo, sozo,* and *diasozo.* Each of these terms signifies the "healing" works of Jesus.

Therapeuo means "to serve," "to do service," "to care for, treat, cure, heal;" "to restore to health." It is the source of the word "therapy." It is used alongside the term for gospelizing in Luke 9:6: "They departed and went through the villages, **bringing the good news** and **curing** diseases everywhere"(emphasis mine). In Luke 7:18-21 and 8:1-3, we find *therapeuo* in the context of Jesus' *gospelizing* (8:21, 22). In Matthew 4:23 and 9:35, the term covers the ability of Jesus to heal all kinds of sicknesses and diseases among the people.

Iaomai means "to cure, heal;" "to make whole;" and is used figuratively of spiritual healing. Jesus spoke about both it and His ministry of gospelizing in Luke 4:18-24. In Acts 10:34-43, both words appear in context, and describe the ministry of Jesus (vv. 36 and 38). *Iaomai* refers to Jesus' power to heal with only "a word" (Luke 7:7, KJV), and to the lepers who were healed by Jesus (17:11-19, v. 15). James 5:16 is a familiar verse where *iaomai* is found: "Therefore confess your sins to one another, and pray for one another, so that you may be **healed**. The prayer of the righteous is powerful and effective" (emphasis mine).

Katharizo means "to make clean, cleanse" and is the source of the word "catharsis." It is used several times to describe the cleansing of lepers, and appears with *gospelize* in Matthew 11:5 and Luke 7:22. In one instance, "2...there was a leper who came to him [Jesus] and knelt before him, saying, 'Lord, if you choose, you can make me **clean**.' [3] He stretched out his hand and touched him, saying, 'I do choose. Be made **clean!**' Immediately his leprosy was **cleansed**" (Matthew 8:2-3, emphasis mine; see also Luke 4:27 and 17:17).

Sozo means "to save;" "keep safe and sound." It means, "to save a suffering one from sickness, disease, and its effects," "to preserve one who is in danger of destruction, to rescue." *Sozo* also is used in the spiritual sense of salvation from sin (cf. 1 Corinthians 15:2, alongside gospelize). In the physical sense we find persons who were made "well" or "whole" by Jesus (Matthew 9:21, 22; Mark 6:56; 10:52; Luke 17:19; Acts 4:9). James 5:15 is familiar: "The prayer of faith will **save** the sick, and the Lord will raise them up; and anyone who has committed sins will be forgiven" (emphasis mine).

Diasozo means "to save; i.e., cure one who is sick, bring him through;" "to save thoroughly." It is found in Matthew 14:36, in which the people brought to Jesus all who were sick, "and begged him that they might touch even the fringe of his cloak; and all who touched it were **healed**" (emphasis mine). In Luke 7:3, a centurion sent for Jesus to come and help his sick servant—to bring him through suffering to healing.

Viewed together, these words are windows into the **holistic healing** brought by Jesus to humanity, and reflect the impartation-authority that Jesus has given to Gospelizers through His Name. Sometimes Jesus healed instantaneously, and sometimes gradually in restoration. In other instances it appears that the healing of Jesus came through the agency of "therapeutic" remedies used in the day. At times, the healings and cures of Jesus also saved the sick from sufferings accompanying their condition. Jesus, of course, made people "whole." On several occasions, the faith of the community and the compassion of Jesus achieved such miraculous results that everybody present received healing.

Holistic Healings of Gospelizers

The holistic healings imparted by Jesus, Who empowered His messengers for the same works, speaks volumes to Gospelizers who would address the HIV/AIDS crisis affecting the contemporary world. Here there is room for seeking cures for the disease; there is room for educational strategies for sexual responsibility; there is room for therapeutic remedies; there is room for the community-wide healing of widows, orphans, and other family members through serving them with family care-giving and safety; there is room for powerful miracles effected by faith and prayer—the "great workings of God." Without question, **there is room for the healing of salvation.** With compassion and courage, Gospelizers can grant hope to those who are dying. We can impart to them the merciful and eternal Gospel of Jesus Christ our Savior. We can spread the Gospel's truth, grace and power before the opportunities pass, before death snatches our precious human harvest into eternity.

Gospelizers Can Proclaim a "Good Word" — Teaching the Black/African Presence in the Bible

Gospelizers have a "good word" to proclaim to people—the truth about the Black and African presence in the Scriptures. Over years of ministry in this area, we have discovered the healing benefits of this word. It serves to heal "the unwell" African psyche which misunderstands the Bible and God, and misreads the place of Black/African people in God's redemption story, past and future. Likewise, "the unwell" non-African psyche, entrenched in racist misunderstanding of the Bible, needs the healing transformation that can come from learning the spiritual truths revealed in the facts about the Black/African Scriptural presence. Let us remember,

"[16] All Scripture is inspired by God and is useful for teaching, for reproof, for correction, and for training in righteousness, [17] so that everyone who belongs to God may be proficient, equipped for every good work." (2 Timothy 3:16-17)

A Response to Racial Terrorism

Detailed identifications of both the historical and cultural African context of the Bible, and notable and numerous persons and nations, are being well established in academic, church, and other settings. Building on this content, we can skillfully use this information to bring healing to countless souls. Due to lack of knowledge, many are perishing from having misread the Bible, the dealings of God with ancient and modern Black people, and the African genealogical, historical, and cultural coming of Jesus into the world. Many are sealing a destiny with eternal condemnation because their terrorizing — bombing churches, preaching racial hatred, burning crosses, and otherwise promoting racial antagonism — is based on misdirected fear of Blacks and misguided ignorance about the world of the Bible. Most of all, they perish from lack of entering into a personal, transformative, and saving relationship with the Lord Christ Jesus, our Savior.

Readers can refer to other sources for a fuller elaboration of this theme.[136] Concisely, there are several specific points to this therapeutic good word for the unenlightened heart and mind. Blacks and whites can gospelize these points for audiences of any race. I have shared with white mission-minded persons several approaches to using these insights when ministering on the mission field to African-descended persons. Several were enlightened and became excited at the potential.[137]

1) Good News! The Black/African physical identity is God-given and gifted. It is fearfully and wonderfully made. It is "black and beautiful."

2) *Good News!* The Black/African standing before God is blessed, not cursed. This humanity has not been, and is not now, the subject of some prejudicial mean-spirited ban, anger, wrath, and judgment of God.

3) *Good News!* The Black/African place in God's redemption story is present from the beginning of history, pervasive throughout, and never marginalized. All humanity shares with them the same need of God's redeeming love.

4) *Good News!* The destiny of God for Black/African humanity in these last days prophesies their role in calling multitudes to Christ by spreading His salvation to "the ends of the earth," and serving a leading role in His Church.

From Mission Ministries to Churches

In the harvest-fields, Gospelizers proceed with several specific aims. Utmost is to bring the salvation of Christ to the lost by gospelizing the good works of Christ, especially among all the least/poor. The good works performed ought to span the holistic spectrum of human need.[138] Through Gospel-centered ministries, germane spiritual, physical, mental, social, and economic concerns should be addressed, even as Christ addressed them.

There are many different manifestations of Christian works that are the fruit of mission. Social ministries of churches are continually springing up. The people of God are initiating a variety of good works. Some churches and church groups have committed themselves to long-term holistic community development.[139] Personal and genuine conversions to Christ are taking place through these services for the Lord. Christ's words are being obeyed and fulfilled: "In the same way, let your light shine before others, so that they may see your good works and give glory to your Father in heaven" (Matthew 5:16).

A third aim flows from the others. An intentional and

spiritually inevitable outcome of accomplishing the two aims should result in **the organization of new churches.** On the one hand, bearing a holistic witness and mission by gospelizing gracious works in Gospel-centered ministries is **necessary.** Yet, on the other hand, multiplying churches, as a gospelizing good work of gathering together believers into Christ's community *(Koinonia)*, is **mandatory.** The first-century church grew by expanding and intensifying its holistic witness, and multiplying into other churches.

The Church is a revelation of the salvation and presence of Christ, and of His community-building work in the world (cf. Ephesians 3:5ff.). Through the Church of the living God, and its manifestation in local congregations, persons saved from sin are also saved from a wicked and evil generation. Those who are saved, having been born anew and "called out" *(ekklesia, "church")* from sin and the world, are also those who have been **called into relationship and fellowship** with one another in the Church, the "Body of Christ," the *Koinonia* (fellowship-community) of which He is the life and Head. Hence, Gospelizers must multiply into additional churches of Christ in order to receive Christian converts into fellowship, and strengthen, care for, and make them into disciples and Gospelizers.

Additionally, there is an overarching reason for seeding new churches: the Church transmits the trust of the Gospel.

The Church's Mission-Purpose

The **mission-purpose** of the Church is to *gospelize* in the Name of Christ with a view toward organizing other churches—insuring in the process that the trust of the Gospel is committed, preserved, and transmitted personally, ethno-culturally, and globally from one generation of Christ's disciples to the next.

11

Multiplying Gospelizers into Churches

> *The Call:*
> •Institute a *Gospelizers'* teaching-discipleship ministry.

Church—The Work of Jesus in the World

Lest we lose sight of our ultimate mission, the Church is called to organize Gospelizers into additional churches! The three-fold ministry makes disciples for Christ, transforms them into Gospelizers, and commissions them into the harvest-fields to give holistic witness to Christ and His Good News. The ministry is completed and perpetuated as groups of Gospelizers are organized into other congregations in the harvest-fields to which they are called and appointed. Making disciples for Jesus Christ reaches full maturity when His followers are called forth as Gospelizers and organized into other churches—other Christian fellowships or congregations.

Jesus said to His followers, "Herein is my Father glorified, **that ye bear much fruit**; so shall ye be my disciples"

(John 15:8, KJV, emphasis mine). Jesus also declared, "You did not choose me but I chose you. And I appointed you to go and bear fruit, **fruit that will last,** so that the Father will give you whatever you ask him in my name" (15:16, emphasis mine). **"Fruit that will last"** is a tacit reference to churches that continue to exist, grow, and reproduce, even despite the homegoings of their members. The Church's eternal existence is assured by Jesus Himself Who said, "...on this rock I will build my church, and the gates of Hades [Hell] will not prevail against it" (Matthew 16:18).

Without question or controversy, the progress and growth of the Church is the highest work of Jesus Christ in our world through His Holy Spirit. Jesus both died and rose for the Church. When Jesus returns, He will return for His Church, for a Bride without spot or wrinkle (cf. Ephesians 5:25-27; Revelation 19:7-9). Throughout all generations the Church shall remain until the Lord returns to fully redeem His Body and Bride!

The Early Church Model

This pattern and ministry of churches growing into additional churches is the Lord's way of adding to and spreading the Church, His Body. This truth is amply demonstrated in the early historical record of the Church found in the book of *Acts*. Our churches should follow this model. We return to a key passage in this discussion, Acts 8:1-4:

> [1] And Saul approved of their killing him [Stephen]. That day a severe persecution began against the church in Jerusalem, and all except the apostles were scattered throughout the countryside of Judea and Samaria. [2] Devout men buried Stephen and made loud lamentation over him. [3] But Saul was ravaging the church by entering house after house; dragging off both men and

women, he committed them to prison. ⁴Now those who were scattered went from place to place, proclaiming *[gospelizing]* the word.

In the midst of terror, the Church grew because the believers did two things. First, they geographically decentralized the Church; they "went from place to place." With the Holy Spirit's boldness and courage, the believers relocated from one place to the next. They did not stay bound to Jerusalem or to their usual meeting places. By terror they were scattered, by choice they pressed their way into new territories. Second, as they decentralized, they gospelized. Everywhere they went they made a holistic witness on their redeeming mission with Jesus. They went heralding the Gospel; they went practicing the Gospel; they went "signing" the Gospel. For example,

> ⁵Philip went down to the city of Samaria and proclaimed *[kerusso]*[140] the Messiah to them. ⁶The crowds with one accord listened eagerly to what was said by Philip, **hearing and seeing the signs that he did,** ⁷for unclean spirits, crying with loud shrieks, came out of many who were possessed; and many others who were paralyzed or lame were cured. ⁸So there was great joy in that city (Acts 8:5-8, emphasis mine).

> But when they believed Philip, who was proclaiming the good news *[gospelizing]* about the kingdom of God and the name of Jesus Christ, they were baptized, both men and women (Acts 8:12).

> Now after Peter and John had testified and spoken the word of the Lord, they returned to Jerusalem, proclaiming the good news *[gospelizing]* to many villages of the Samaritans (Acts 8:25).

> Then Philip began to speak, and starting with this

scripture [Isaiah 53:7-8], he proclaimed to him [the Ethiopian Eunuch] the good news *[gospelized]* about Jesus (Acts 8:35).

But Philip found himself at Azotus, and as he was passing through the region, he proclaimed the good news *[gospelized]* to all the towns until he came to Caesarea (Acts 8:40).

In Her earliest development, the Church grew by expanding and intensifying its witness, and growing those who were converted into other churches.[141] Baptism signified inclusion into the local congregation. The formation of additional churches was the commandment and continuing work that Jesus gave through the Holy Spirit to empower His Church in this mission.[142] For instance,

Meanwhile **the church** throughout Judea, Galilee, and Samaria had peace and was built up. Living in the fear of the Lord and in the comfort of the Holy Spirit, **it increased in numbers** (Acts 9:31, emphasis mine).

And after they had appointed **elders for them in each church,** with prayer and fasting they entrusted them to the Lord in whom they had come to believe (Acts 14:23, emphasis mine).

Naturalizing Spiritual Activity

Following the pattern of the early Church, the clear ministry of any specific church should be to organize additional church groups as the natural spiritual outgrowth of its own membership. This mission work should become the passion of each and all believers who desire the growth of the Church—the expansion of their own local congregation, as well as the growth of the Church as a whole—the universal Body of Christ.

When Gospelizers grow and organize other churches, they are doing the basic ministry of any particular church or body of believers. No other mission or ministry is more important or essential for any church. Whatever else is done, the mission of any congregation ought to be aimed at making disciples of the Lord among all nations of the world, by organizing matured *Gospelizers* from its ranks into other Christian fellowships. This ministry is basic.[143]

The growth of additional congregations from an existing church is, or should be, spiritually natural. Church growth inevitably takes place whenever and wherever three things happen: 1) people get saved; 2) they spiritually grow or mature together; and 3) they are called by the Holy Spirit to gospelize in another place, thus extending the Body of Christ to all humanity, throughout the world.

Growing Orderly or Disorderly Churches

The Church must and will grow. Jesus' parables of *The Mustard Seed* and *The Yeast* affirm Church growth.[144] However, there are two alternatives: either the Church will **grow in an orderly manner** or She will **grow in a disorderly manner**. At any rate, **the Church will grow!** For Christ will see to it that the Church grows! For Christ is the Head of the Church, and it is Christ Himself Who grows or builds the Church, which is His Body.

When there is no orderly program for the growth of a church, that church tends to grow disorderly. Consequently, either unrest and disharmony take hold in the congregation, or the church divides or splits. It is better to arrange orderly growth for our churches. Planning for the organization of committed members and mature leaders into other churches is preferred over experiencing the disharmonious spirit, and/or movement of justifiably discontented disciples from one church into another.

On orderly church growth, we have the following words of the Apostle Paul written to Titus, one of Paul's special messengers. "I left you behind in Crete for this reason, so that you should put in order what remained to be done, and should appoint elders in every town, as I directed you" (Titus 1:5).

Confirming Gospelizers as Church-Planters

> [1] Now in the church at Antioch there were prophets and teachers: Barnabas, Simeon who was called Niger, Lucius of Cyrene, Manaen a member of the court of Herod the ruler, and Saul. [2] While they were worshiping the Lord and fasting, the Holy Spirit said, "Set apart for me Barnabas and Saul for the work to which I have called them." [3] Then after fasting and praying they laid their hands on them and sent them off. [4] So, being sent out by the Holy Spirit, they went down to Seleucia; and from there they sailed to Cyprus. [5] When they arrived at Salamis, they proclaimed the word of God in the synagogues of the Jews. And they had John also to assist them (Acts 13:1-5).

We receive help by understanding this record of the church at Antioch, and the Holy Spirit's role in calling forth the Lord's messengers into His harvest. Gospelizing church-planters need confirmation. Not everyone is called or is equipped for this mission work. Gospelizers who organize into churches should be *Spirit-called, Spirit-led, and competent in the ministry*.

Barnabas was ready; Saul (Paul) was ready. These spiritually attuned Jewish brothers — along with several other ethnically diverse and Black believers in the Church[145] — were prepared and willing to serve Christ on the mission-field. They evidenced gifts of prophecy and teaching; they were worshiping the Lord, fasting and praying. They were sensitive to the voice of the Holy Spirit. They were able to spiritually discern from among the many members in the congregation specifically whom the

Lord had already called.[146] They understood the mission work of the Lord. They knew to pray for confirmation before making any moves. In affirmation they were obedient to and co-workers with the Spirit of God. They knew the power and effectual work of "the laying on of the hands." And they knew how to supportively send good men to go where the Lord was leading them.

Saul and Barnabas were obedient to the call of the Spirit. **"So, being sent out by the Holy Spirit, they went...and...proclaimed the word of God..."** (Acts 13:4a, 5b, emphasis mine). (Remember the words Jesus spoke to His disciples, "Peace be with you. As the Father has sent me, so I send you" (John 20:21).) The Holy Spirit is a gospelizing Spirit. Jesus proclaimed, **"The Spirit of the Lord** is upon me, because he has anointed me to bring good news *[gospelize]* to the poor" (Luke 4:18, emphasis mine). The Apostle Peter wrote,

> It was revealed to them [the prophets] that they were serving not themselves but you [Peter's readers], in regard to the things that have now been announced to you through those who brought you good news *[gospelized you]* by **the Holy Spirit** sent from heaven—things into which angels long to look! (1 Peter 1:12, emphasis mine)[147]

The gospelizing Holy Spirit called the transformed disciples, the Church confirmed them, and the mission-team went as directed. They went forth as Gospelizers. And as Gospelizers on a Spirit-led campaign, they organized church after church after church. The Church grew and continued to grow.[148]

We should mark well the calling of Paul and Barnabas, and the confirmation pattern of this genuinely spiritual community of predominantly African-descended believers. By heeding the voice of God the Holy Spirit they demonstrated that they were co-workers with the Lord in

His work of gospelizing. Imitating them, let us also joy-fully and spontaneously submit to the Holy Spirit by confirming and sending gospelizing church-planters into the harvest-fields. "19 Do not quench the Spirit. 20 Do not despise the words of prophets" (1 Thessalonians 5:19-20).

The Church's Mission-Purpose

The **mission-purpose** of the Church is to gospelize in the Name of Christ with a view toward organizing other churches—insuring in the process that the trust of the Gospel is committed, preserved, and transmitted personally, ethno-culturally, and globally from one generation of Christ's disciples to the next.

12

Structuring Churches

The Call:
- **Organize *Gospelizers* into churches.**

Churches should organize Gospelizers into churches. This ministry should neither be accidental nor exceptional. Organizing other churches is an act of gospelizing, and a response to the fruit of holistic outreach and growth of church membership. This strategy is also a viable alternative, helping our churches resist an often debilitating and sidetracking "a bigger building is better" mentality.

Gospelizers initiate their work as messengers connected to the church that commissioned them. The work of some Gospelizers will naturally point in the direction of new churches. As the opportunity presents itself, these Gospelizers should be organized into new congregations.[149]

The way gospelizing churches are structured will contribute to the effectiveness of their ministry. Success in the Gospelizers' ministry hinges on whether **first things are kept first.** Once our values are determined and prioritized, we must adhere to and guard them tenaciously.

Constant Priorities

The teaching-discipleship ministry that inspires the movement into gospelizing is the same ministry that sets the priorities for a church. Gospelizing churches should maintain several essential priorities. Each flows from the mission-purpose of the Church, restated here:

The Church's Mission-Purpose

The **mission-purpose** of the Church is to gospelize in the Name of Christ with a view toward organizing other churches — insuring in the process that the trust of the Gospel is committed, preserved, and transmitted personally, ethno-culturally, and globally from one generation of Christ's disciples to the next.

This purpose is the highest calling of Christian stewardship in the context of the Church's mission. There are seven priorities related to this mission-purpose that a good and faithful church should maintain at the highest level: [150]

Seven Essential Priorities for Churches

1) *Gospelize in the Name of Christ*

2) *Baptize Converts to Christ*

3) *Commune in the Supper of Christ*

4) *Worship God as Revealed in Christ*

5) *Perform the Studied Word of Christ*

6) *Fellowship and Pray with the People of Christ*

7) *Multiply Churches of Christ*

A Scriptural basis exists for each of these priorities.

1) GOSPELIZE in the Name of Christ

Gospelizing is the essence of Christian witness, and the key to growing an effective and Christ-honoring church. A church full of Gospelizers should continually give holistic witness by performing everything from communicating the word of salvation to the lost, to demonstrating gracious works, to making people whole, to providing the *Koinonia*, to fighting ungodly societal systems, and to growing churches everywhere. Personally and collectively the ministry of Gospelizers finds them witnessing and evangelizing, preaching and heralding the good word of salvation, performing great workings of healing and deliverance, doing good and gracious works, ministering to the "least of these," bringing about Christ's "Jubilee," destroying the "gates of hell," fighting for the righteous causes of the powerless, poor, and afflicted, and manifesting other acts of gospelizing.

Collectively, the Church gives a holistic witness for the Lord. In doing so, Gospelizers become all things to all people; so that by all means some can be saved. Gospelizers serve human needs, renew genuine community, and work to reconstruct a better society in order to save the lost, to convert the sinner to Christ for the glory of God (cf. Luke 4:18; Mark 16:15-20; Matthew 5:13-16; 12:15-23; 28:18-20; Luke 8:1-3; Acts 4:33; 5:12-16; 1 Corinthians 9:19-23; 10:31 – 11:1; Titus 3:1-8).

2) BAPTIZE Converts to Christ

The Church should administer water baptism to those who convert to Christ. Baptism primarily signifies disciple-commitment to Jesus. It also is the way converts are *"Koinonia-ized,"* or included in a local church. Baptism publicly demonstrates a believer's union with Christ—a union with the Lord in His death/burial to sin, and in His life/resurrection to God (cf. Acts 2:37-42; Romans 6:1ff.).

3) COMMUNE in the Supper of Christ

The Church must always **remember Jesus** by communing in the Lord's Supper: "the bread" and "the cup" that signify the body and the blood of Jesus. Holy Communion is a membership right, a personal responsibility, and a God-granted privilege of every baptized believer in Christ. The Communion affirms the presence of Christ with His followers, and the reality and fellowship of the Church, Christ's Body, the *Koinonia*. Further, the Lord's Supper proclaims the death of Christ until the resurrected Lord returns. It celebrates the atoning sacrifice Christ made for sinners on Calvary's cross (cf. Acts 2:42; 1 Corinthians 11:23-26ff.).

4) WORSHIP GOD as Revealed in Christ

The Church is a worshiping congregation.[151] We worship God as revealed in Christ. Christ has "exegeted" the Father, making us to know the true nature of God.[152] God is Spirit, a true and living God. He is seeking those who worship Him in Spirit and in truth (cf. Luke 24:50-53; John 1:18; 4:19-24; Acts 2:47).

5) PERFORM the Studied Word of Christ

The Church is accountable to God for living the studied word of Christ. We are not merely hearers of the word, but doers. We hear and study the Word of God so that we may perform those things of God expected of Christ's followers.[153] The early Church devoted itself to the teachings of Christ passed on and explained to them by the apostles. They practiced and actualized the words of Jesus and the truth of His teachings (cf. Colossians 3:15-17; Acts 2:42).

6) FELLOWSHIP and PRAY with the People of Christ

The Church of Christ is a fellowship; the *Koinonia*; the community of Christ's Body. The people of God are connected and in spiritual relationship with each another. The early Church devoted themselves to the community-family of believers, especially caring for each another. Prayer was integral to the fellowship. Often the Church prayed together. As a spiritually connected and common fellowship they collectively poured out both their praises and their problems to the Lord (cf. Acts 2:42, 46; 4:23-31).

7) MULTIPLY CHURCHES of Christ

The Church gave birth to "churches." The careful student of Scripture notices the back and forth reference to the "church" (singular), to "churches" (plural), and to "each church" (particular).[154] There is only one Church, the Body of Christ, uniting together each and all believers in all times. However, there are numerous "churches," that is, congregations of believers. Each church possesses the full presence of Christ and the nature of the Church as a whole.

Christ the Head of the Church, through His Gospelizers, continues to produce and multiply His Body into other churches. The same work of Christ begun more than 2000 years ago continues in our generation. Christ forms the spiritual nature of our churches into additional congregations of believers. As co-workers in cooperation with our Lord and His will for church growth, we should submit to the reproductive work of God. Each church of Christ ought to grow some churches for Christ (cf. John 15:8, 15-17; Acts 9:31; 14:23; 15:4, 40-41; 16:4-5; Romans 16:4-5, 16; 1 Corinthians 4:17).

The aim of all church activity and programs should lead God's people toward the objective of growing additional churches by organizing Gospelizers. Everything done by a church should be done to the glory of God. God receives the highest glory when Gospel proclamation saves the lost; when the saved get *Koinonia-ized* and discipled into Christ; when Christ's disciples do holistic gospelizing in the harvest-fields, and when Gospelizers multiply by growing themselves together with new converts into additional churches!

Structure, Service Areas, Operational Groups, and Servant-Leaders

In the following section four points are considered: *the "Church-in-Progress" structure, the core areas of service, operational groups,* and *the character of servant-leaders.* These ideas are best received when understood in the context of the constant priorities explained above.

"Church-in-Progress" Structure

Leaders who function in the capacity of pastoral headship of our several congregations—indeed serving as the under-shepherds of Jesus Christ, the Great Head of the Church—should consider structuring their church membership and programs toward the aim of developing additional churches. So organized, church members as cell-groups will become the "Church-in-Progress."

The Church-in-Progress organization will become seeds of the Body of Christ, which Christ eventually will plant in other places in our communities and throughout the world. Church planting will come about when Gospelizers 1) have spiritually matured, 2) have been called out by the Lord for forming another church wherever He leads them in His harvest-field, and 3) have been set apart by the Holy Spirit, affirmed, and commissioned through the Church for this purpose.

Constant priorities of the ministry (explained earlier) should shape the Church-in-Progress structure. Jesus taught

His followers that new wine demands new wineskins (cf. Luke 6:37-38). It is well not to ignore the implications of this teaching when implementing a church-planting strategy of ministry, especially if we desire to become most effective and fruitful. Certain old practices, programmatic traditions, and outmoded forms of church organization cannot contain and usefully serve the ministry of strategically preparing Gospelizers to organize into churches.[155] The way our churches are structured must naturally feed into the ministry of church-planting.

Core Areas of Service

Several core areas of service should become the backbone of the Church-in-Progress organization. That is, each member of the church should serve in one of the following areas. Each of those areas should focus on a specific teaching-discipleship training and on showing the relationship of the particular to the whole. Each Church-in-Progress should have a core group of leaders who will serve the Body in these areas. Let's consider these core areas of service.

Servants OVER the Church

There are two areas for ordering the Church, identified as Biblical officers: pastoral overseers and deacon/deaconess servers.

1) **Pastoral Overseers** are the ministers (elders and bishops) of the church. They shepherd the flock, oversee the work, and maintain the vision of Christ for His people.

2) **Deacon/Deaconess Servers** specialize in serving the church. They assist, care for, and free up the Pastoral Overseers so that the latter can concentrate on what they are especially called and gifted to do. Deacons/ Deaconesses also oversee the provision for the poor, needy, and afflicted (cf. Acts 6:1-7).

Servants IN the Church

There are four areas for edifying the Church: worship leaders, teachers-leadership developers, fellowship caretakers, and membership gatekeepers.

1) Worship Leaders inspire, coordinate, and guide truthful and spiritual worship.

2) Teachers/Leadership Developers concentrate on teaching the Word and feeding the flock. They are responsible for forming and organizing the catechism content and teaching the church's truths and principles. Chiefly, they make disciples for Christ, and identify and develop teaching-leaders throughout the Church (cf. 2 Timothy 2:2).

3) Fellowship Caretakers attend to the *Koinonia*, the fellowship of the Church and the ongoing experience and strengthening of the Body. They minister to the special needs of the saints: the blessing of children, marriage ceremonies, home-goings, and overall triumphs and tragedies.

4) Membership Gatekeepers concern themselves with admission, restoration, and discipline of church members. In this capacity they prepare converts and others for membership; they "wash the saints' feet" (cf. John 13:14); they admonish and administer corrective action where necessary. Also, they protectively guard the Body, acting as "watchpersons on the wall," "gatekeepers," and "doorkeepers" in the house of the Lord.

Servants FROM the Church

Two areas are necessary for gospelizing the world: Gospelizers as social activists, and Gospelizers as church-planters.

1) Gospelizers as Social Activists manifest corporately the good works of Christ, the gospelizing ministry of Jubilee (cf. Luke 4:16-21). They serve the "poor and afflicted," "the least of these," in proclaiming, healing, and delivering in areas of social righteousness, justice, and peace.

2) Gospelizers as Church-Planters are the organizers and growers of additional churches. When called by the Holy Spirit, they go forth into new areas where the impact of the Gospel is not evident. And they go forth as the Body of Christ, the Church.

Servants FOR the Church

There are two areas of service useful for satisfying the requirements of government and society: they are trustees and administrating managers.

1) Trustees are required for our churches, due to the legal system of our society. As such, "trustees" were nonexistent in the early Church. Church members brought their monies and resources, and laid them at the apostles' feet (Acts 4:37). The apostles, in turn, told the church to select certain trustworthy believers who would essentially serve the widows (Acts 6:1-7). Thus, the stewardship of the churches' material resources fell within the purview of ministers and deacons/deaconesses. In this light, trustees' primary role is to insure that the church remains on good legal footing within society, so as not to have its ministry impeded. Thus, trustees act as stewards of the Church's material assets in a legal and civic context.

2) Administrating Managers are closely aligned with the trustees, and mind the church business and operational affairs. They primarily address administrative matters that maintain efficiency of church functions.

```
┌─────────────────────────────────────────┐
│          10 Core Areas of Service        │
│                 of the                   │
│       Church-in-Progress Structure       │
│                                          │
│           1) Pastoral Overseers          │
│        2) Deacon & Deaconess Servers     │
│            3) Worship Leaders            │
│     4) Teachers/Leadership Developers    │
│          5) Fellowship Caretakers        │
│         6) Membership Gatekeepers        │
│       7) Gospelizing Social Activists    │
│       8) Gospelizing Church-Planters     │
│                9) Trustees               │
│        10) Administrative Managers       │
└─────────────────────────────────────────┘
```

Operational Groups — Churches in Preparation

In addition to every church member participating in one of the ten core areas of service, each member should also be assigned to a Church-in-Progress operational group. Each operational group should contain at least ten persons — one from each core area of service. Thus, the essential members for organizing a church and doing holistic gospelizing ministry will be present in any given Church-in-Progress group. Under this structure, each group has the necessary people to serve all essential Biblical areas of the Church's ministry, and will be able to fulfill the seven essential priorities related to the Church's mission-purpose. Ideally, each Church-in-Progress group will be prepared to function as a new church on its own when and if the Spirit sends them forth on this mission.

Refer to the following illustration.

A Church-in-Progress
Operational Group

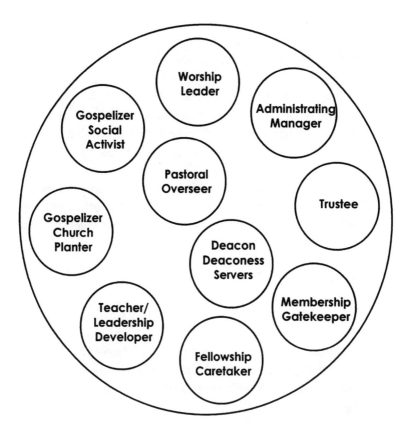

Each operational group has at least ten members;
one representative from
each core service area of the Church.

Character of Servant-Leaders

Jesus was a servant, and taught His followers to be the same. He said,

> 42 ..."You know that among the Gentiles those whom they recognize as their rulers lord it over them, and their great ones are tyrants over them. 43 But it is not so among you; but whoever wishes to become great among you must be your servant, 44 and whoever wishes to be first among you must be slave of all. 45 For the Son of Man came not to be served but to serve, and to give his life a ransom for many" (Mark 10:42b-45).

As servant-leaders, Gospelizers should have six essential qualities of character: *spiritual maturity, gifted activity, discipling ability, a warrior's mentality, flexible availability,* and *compassionate personality.*

Servant-Leaders must demonstrate:

1) *Spiritual Maturity – 1 Corinthians 3:1-3*

Spiritual maturity is Christ-centered developed character. There are three kinds of Christians. There are "babes" in Christ, persons who have recently taken Christ the Lord as their Savior. There are "carnal" Christians, believers controlled by ungodly principles and values. And there are "spiritual" believers, those who are being filled with the Spirit and who are developing Christ-likeness in all of life. Gospelizers have grown to spiritual maturity.

2) *Gifted Activity – Romans 12:3-8; Ephesians 4:11-16; 1 Corinthians 12:4-11; 12:27 – 13:3; 1 Peter 4:10-11*

Gifted activity describes those believers who understand and appreciate the gifts of the Holy Spirit in the

Church. They use their own personal gifts in the service of the Lord and in fellowship with the Body. They recognize that God grows and works in and through His Church through believers exercising Spiritual gifts. The emphasis here is on the supernatural manifestation of God in the inter-relations and activities of the Church.

3) *Discipling Ability – 1 Corinthians 3:10-15; Ephesians 4:12*

Discipling ability draws attention to equipping the saints for the work of the ministry. Transmitting the Gospel to the next generation of Christ's disciples is the aim. Believers holding a leadership position in the church must prove their own capability in making disciples. They should be able to bring another person to spiritual maturity in the ways and works of Christ, not just to train another Christian in some aspect of church work. They each must demonstrate the ability to "enable" other church members to fulfill Christ's mission.

4) *A Warrior's Mentality – Matthew 16:16-18; Ephesians 6:10-18; 1 Timothy 1:18; 6:12; Hebrews 2:14-15; 1 John 3:8; 5:4-5*

A warrior's mentality calls believers to fight the good fight of the Christian faith. This mind-set accepts the Christ-defined militant posture of the Church. Jesus said of the Church, "...the gates of hell shall not prevail against it" (Matthew 16:18, KJV). Gospelizers are soldiers of Christ. Christians must wage warfare in the Name of Christ, and believers should demonstrate their fitness for battle in all the serving, planting, working, and building they do.[156]

5) Flexible Availability – Philippians 1:21; 1 Corinthians 9:19-23

Flexible availability is required of Christ's servants who lead the Church. A wise deacon remarked: "When working for the Lord, we always have steady work, but we don't always know where the job will be!"[157] The goal here is to use leaders who have freedom to serve Christ and His Church, and who demonstrate adaptability to changing circumstances and unexpected challenges. Christians may be blessed with all the best gifts and potential. However, if they are not available, their gifts and potential mean little for the advancement of the Church. Christ's Gospelizers show availability to commit time, energy, and resources.

6) Compassionate Personality – Mark 6:30-34ff.

Compassionate personality is the manifestation of warm and caring love and support, especially for the suffering. Leaders in the Church should be persons of compassion. This is especially so for Gospelizers. They must respond to the suffering masses as Jesus responded. When the Lord saw the masses "he had compassion for them, because they were like sheep without a shepherd; and he began to teach them many things" (Mark 6:34). And after the Lord compassionately taught them, He also fed them (cf. Mark 6:35ff.). When church leaders show compassion they draw those who are suffering to Jesus. An uncaring coldness drives people away from the Lord and His Church.[158]

13

Maximizing Resources

The Call:

• **Maximize resources for the *Gospelizers'* ministry.**

This call challenges each church to:

a. Rework schedules and programs around daily and seasonal gospelizing.

b. Allocate funds and receive special offerings for supporting Gospelizers and their ministry, programs, and activities. Shift certain monies from unnecessary building and capital improvement campaigns to the gospelizing ministry.

c. Make full use of the total space in all existing facilities, including the often underused worship sanctuary.

Adhering to these practices will keep our churches free to do outreach and attain church growth.

Invest in Gospelizers

People invest in what they believe. When believers and churches believe in Gospelizers and their ministry, the resources will show it. These resources are time, seasons, and program; human and financial; and property.

Time, Season, and Program Resources

Chapter 2 emphasized the importance of giving urgent daily time to the ministry of gospelizing. Seasonal and annual dimensions of time are also important considerations. Believers and our churches must grapple with these dimensions in fulfilling the gospelizing mission. In fact, one's calling and mission in Christ should become one's total life. Gospelizing characterized the whole life and ministry of Christ (cf. Ephesians 2:17; Acts 10:36). Paul testified, "For to me, living is Christ and dying is gain" (Philippians 1:21). The annual church calendar should reflect a church's priority and time commitment in the context of the gospelizing ministry.

Calendar of Commitment

Arranging the Yearly Calendar

How does a gospelizing church arrange its yearly calendar? What should become its month-by-month rhythm? These are important questions in light of the several imperatives of Gospelizers. We call our churches to be open daily, and to reach out as never before. Obviously, such a program demands careful consideration and planning, lest it begin to work against the overall purpose.

Senior Pastors should broaden their church's preaching, teaching, and leadership ministry. Is it wise for a pastor to do the preaching at two or three Sunday services of the church? What should be done about weekly services? Of necessity, pastors must fashion a Church-in-Progress leadership structure differently than typical church leadership models.

Some kind of rotating schedule seems required if the ministry of gospelizing churches is to take hold. After all, Jesus (and His disciples) often withdrew from the continuous demands of ministry for times of prayer and personal renewal. Implementing some kind of Sabbath-Jubilee schedule would assist Gospelizers and the growth of gospelizing churches.

A suggested rotation would consist of six weeks of creative mission work, and one week for celebration and renewal, for a total rotation period of 42 weeks (six cycles). Then the seventh period (weeks 43-49) would be for reflection and renewal. Week 50 would be the Jubilee, a special celebration of the ministry accomplishments during the year. During Jubilee emphasis should be placed on empowering the poor and thanking the Lord for the grace and freedom of His Gospel. The final two weeks of the year could be set aside for strategic planning. This kind of calendar year would look something like the following.

A *Gospelizers'*
Sabbath-Jubilee Calendar Year

Cycle	*Weeks*		*Activity*
1	1-6		Creative Mission Work
		7	Celebration/Renewal
2	8-13		Creative Mission Work
		14	Celebration/Renewal
3	15-20		Creative Mission Work
		21	Celebration/Renewal
4	22-27		Creative Mission Work
		28	Celebration/Renewal
5	29-34		Creative Mission Work
		35	Celebration/Renewal
6	36-41		Creative Mission Work
		42	Celebration/Renewal
7	43-49		Reflection & Renewal
		50	**JUBILEE**
		51-52	Strategic Planning

Any church calendar has its challenges, especially for churches that maintain intensive outreach ministries. The above suggestion is no exception. In order to stay focused on the mission of gospelizing, churches will need to address several issues, such as:

How will the church maintain a continuous (a 24/7) operation under a Sabbath-Jubilee rotation schedule?

How does inter-church fellowship affect such a schedule of ministry?

What place do the Holy Days of the Christian calendar have in this schedule?

What about national/cultural holidays? How will they be handled?

How will the calendar address denominational churches that have district, state, and national conventions and congresses?

In what ways should the rotation apply to church leaders versus the members?

How should the schedule incorporate aspects of accountability with individual freedom and flexibility?

How should the schedule be adjusted for church or national crises?

Most of the answers to those questions emerge from the church's strategic planning times. Conflicts in scheduling always arise. The aim is to insure that when conflicts occur, persons responsible for maintaining the vision do so. Matters and activities of lesser importance must not displace and derail the church's essential mission of gospelizing.

A Church-Planting Strategic Plan and Program

Many churches have developed their strategic plans covering any number of years: Having planned their work, these congregations have committed themselves to working their plan. Many of these plans deal with building another structure to house the church and its programs. The assumption is that a church can do a greater ministry with better facilities. However, what greater ministry is there than supporting Gospelizers in their mission, whether overseas or at home? What greater ministry is there than spreading the church through evangelism and seeding new congregations?

A church's strategic plan should reflect the witness and mission of Gospelizers, especially as it relates to planting new congregations. The questions for a church then become:

- How many new churches do we have the capacity to organize each year for the next ten years?

- How many Gospelizers can we support (in Africa, Asia, Brazil, or Europe, etc.) for the next ten years until the churches they seed are self-supporting?

- By what strategies can we intensively blanket our community with the Gospel during a three-year period and in such a way that the majority of residents, workers, visitors, or passersby will have the opportunity to hear Christ's Good News and respond to His invitation?

- What "gracious works" can we do that are the most effective forms of social witness for drawing community residents to Christ and His Church?

If gospelizing does not enter the plan, most likely it will be neglected. The call here is for our churches to develop a strategic plan that is thoroughly driven by the *Gospelizers'* mission, and is clear enough and specific enough to be understood, achieved, and assessed. This is not asking too much. After all, when the agenda fits our personal preferences, we often manage to assert and create a program we can implement. Why not design a plan for a gospelizing program that leads to church-planting?[159]

Human and Financial Resources

Mission needs Gospelizers, and gospelizing requires **money.** Churches and believers who truly believe in the ministry of Gospelizers will support their work.

As discussed in chapters 9 and 10, our churches need to identify Gospelizers who are called and competent, and then commission them to do their work for Christ. A number of our churches contain "leaders-in-waiting." However, many of them are waiting for another church to become vacant of a pastor; or sadly, they're waiting for the opportunity when their own pastor goes home to be with the Lord. What a waste of God's human resources. If potential leaders have been "called," why not commission several of them as Gospelizers, assign them a field to gospelize and/or empower them to organize a new congregation, support them for a season, and see what happens?

There are other wasted resources in and around our churches. Not all are formal ministers or called to church-planting. There are men and women—including young adult men and women—who desire to serve the Lord full-time and life-long. However, because of financial responsibilities they must give the best of their time and energies to secular occupations.[160]

What types of ministries can our churches do to rechannel the gifts and talents of young adults into the ministry of gospelizing? Suggestions include supporting short-term (for three months) missionary workers in Africa and other places; establishing night-time street ministry; doing intensive child support and evangelism classes before or after school or on Saturdays; organizing and overseeing music and dance ministries for children and teenagers; doing follow-through ministry for converts by making home visitations and one-to-one discipleship. The Lord will provide creative and effective ideas for those churches that show their willingness to gospelize by enlisting human resources and giving financial support.

The women mentioned in Luke 8:1-3 are a paradigm of financial support for Gospelizers. The Word tells us that these women "provided for them [Jesus and His disciples] out of their resources" (v. 3b). These women served as "patrons" for Jesus and His disciples **as they all were *gospelizing*.** They believed in the mission, for they were recipients of its blessings and accompanied Jesus. Evidently the women had the means to maintain a good amount of "disposable income." Or perhaps some of their husbands financially supported them (cf. "Joanna, the wife of Herod's steward Chuza," v. 3a). At any rate, they were sufficiently independent, proactive, and mission minded both to spend time traveling with Jesus and serve as financial supporters of the gospelizing ministry. See, also, Romans 16:1-2, in which Paul commends the supportive work of Phoebe, a deaconess of the church at Cenchreae.

The work of Gospelizers in our day requires the same kind of monetary commitment to the ministry. The support of Joanna, Susanna, and other women is an outstanding model that all of us would do well to emulate, if we are financially able.

The Philippian church provides another model, that of **partnership** *(koinonia)* in the Gospel. Paul wrote to them,

> ³ I thank my God every time I remember you, ⁴ constantly praying with joy in every one of my prayers for all of you, ⁵ because of your **sharing in** the gospel from the first day until now (Philippians 1:3-5, emphasis mine).

And,

> ¹⁵ You Philippians indeed know that in the early days

of the gospel, when I left Macedonia, no church **shared with me in the matter of giving and receiving,** except you alone. For even when I was in Thessalonica, you sent me help for my needs more than once (Philippians 4:15-16, emphasis mine).

Our churches must financially partner with the Gospelizers' ministry. The relationship must be reciprocal, that of "giving and receiving." Just as the Philippian church supported the work of the Apostle Paul, so too must our churches support those missionaries who do the work of Christ in other places of our world. Jesus said, "It is more blessed to give than to receive" (Acts 20:35).

It has been noted that a church is well on its way in the work of mission when the church maintains a single consolidated budget, **and the mission budget in fact becomes the church budget!**[161] Every programmatic item of the church's ministry should be mission-oriented. The church budget must reflect this reality. After all, if the church is not head-over-foot into missions, then what in the world for Christ is it doing?

Wouldn't it be creative for a church to shift, say $125,000, from its stored-up "building" or "capital improvement" fund, in order to support four additional full-time mission-workers as Gospelizers of the church? The converts to Christ and resulting church members that a four-member crew of Gospelizers could gain in one year could be tremendous. And the financial returns could be surprising. Nevertheless, what financial price could any of us place on a single soul brought to Christ?

Not all Gospelizers are waiting for a church to financially support them. Instead, they are "tent-makers;" they are already supporting themselves and, of their own leading and choice, are giving themselves to the work of the ministry. However, they still need to receive focus and a direction so their gifts can be fully employed by the church.

An Alternative—Shift funds to gospelizing

Suppose there is a church that is growing, "busting at the seams" with members. Their present facility is used to capacity, every day of the week. Suppose an opportunity arises to buy or build a facility four times as large as the present building. Suppose money is not an obstacle because the members are giving their tithes and offerings abundantly. Suppose they make financial projections and determine that they can sustain a $20,000/month note for the next ten years while quadrupling their space.

What if that church decides not to expand their property? Instead, they decide to decentralize and multiply their ministry into new congregations. What if they use the $20,000 per month to support Gospelizers in their mission? What if?!

Jesus said, "For where your treasure is, there your heart will be also" (Luke 12:34).

Property Resources

Maximizing Ministry and Multiplying Churches: An Alternative to Mega-sizing and Unnecessary Construction

What does a church do when it *thinks* it is outgrowing its facility? Usually, following the current trend (and seeking to keep up with the "Joneses") the church plans to build another facility. Many leaders possess a mentality of "mega-sizing" church facilities, placing more emphasis on "brick and mortar," rather than on people and outreach.

Ironically, a church may feel it needs more and better space for ministry; yet its current programs are not operating daily, and are not functioning full-time throughout each day. There is the felt need for a larger capacity sanctuary,[162] yet there may be only one or two Sunday worship services. For the rest of Sunday and throughout the week, except on special occasions, the sanctuary is rarely used.

Most members become sedentary and outreach-stagnant, expending much of their energy and monies on the "building program." Organizing a second congregation to ease overcrowding especially on Sunday is seemingly never considered as a viable outreach alternative to the structure-building program.

We must rethink our assumptions—associating more or better material possessions and buildings with the fullness of Christian ministry. (There are a number of churches with large buildings but relatively few members; many churches of this nature in Europe are more on the order of "museums.") Have we forgotten the experiences of God's power and provision in growing His work and meeting people's needs, despite the humble places and meager resources at hand? A church-leadership mentality that says, "...godliness is a means of [material] gain," is the elusive and unspiritual pursuit of the values of materialism. Genuine spirituality, the highest values of the kingdom, and the blessings of spiritual pursuits are found elsewhere.

Here is a challenging question:

> **Why is it necessary to build a bigger building when for an alternative a church could just as well maximize the use of its present resources, or organize another congregation to effectively multiply and spread Christ's Good News and Church into other areas, near and far?**[163]

I believe Christ is calling the Church away from megasizing and geographical centralization, which can bottleneck the ministry. He is calling the Church to maximization of resources and broad multiplication of churches. Our pastoral leaders should diversify their pastoral functions relative to service in the church.[164] Teamwork is the need of the ministry. Further, church leadership should then work to decentralize from a sole place, in order to form other congregations.

Pastoral leaders (or church boards) can prevent fear of losing membership control by recognizing that only Jesus is the Owner and LORD of the Church; only the Holy Spirit is the power of the Church; only the Scriptures are the final authority in the Church. Stewardship over the Church is one thing. Domineering the Church, replacing Christ as the center of the Church's life and work, is quite another. In this sense, "controlling" the Church and effectively gospelizing the harvest-fields of the world cannot co-exist.

The decentralization of believers into the work of additional Christian congregations is preferable over the massive, centralized controlling organization on the order of a mega-corporate structure. In situations where God has blessed pastors with mega-churches—praise Him, and so be it.[165] The rest of us should turn our sails in a different direction. Let us remember that the desired goal is to achieve the type of Church growth that can be measured by winning new converts to Christ, maximizing outreach ministry, and multiplying new congregations in the harvest-fields. This is the essence of gospelizing.

The spiritual winds of the Holy Spirit are calling for us in our churches—under Christ, competent leaders, and the grace of God—to organize Gospelizers into new churches. He is compelling us to support these churches, and to set them free for Christ Himself to Head, lead, and grow. Christ desires to take these new churches with Him in gospelizing, and to eventually multiply them into more congregations as they too are transformed into His Gospelizers![166]

Postscript:

The Righteous and Joyful Worship
of Gospelizers

Without Gospelizers, worship of God becomes
profane, hypocritical, and socially pacifying.

Gospelizers are the cyclical path from joyful worship to
community ministry and back to joyful worship!

Joyful Worshipers

It is difficult to escape notice of the joyful worship of
Gospelizers described in the Scriptures. As Christ's disciples were transformed into Gospelizers and performed the
righteous work of their commission, joy began to fill their
experience. The spirit of praise and glory in God transformed their worship. No wonder, for the same joy of
worship manifested itself in the life of our Lord as He did
the work of a Gospelizer. In the Scriptures we see this
worship in the joyful experience of Jesus, His disciples/
apostles, and others.

Jesus – Luke 10:21-24

21 At that same hour Jesus rejoiced in the Holy Spirit
and said, "I thank you, Father, Lord of heaven and
earth, because you have hidden these things from the
wise and the intelligent and have revealed them to infants; yes, Father, for such was your gracious will.
22 All things have been handed over to me by my Father; and no one knows who the Son is except the
Father, or who the Father is except the Son and anyone to

whom the Son chooses to reveal him." ²³ Then turning to the disciples, Jesus said to them privately, "Blessed are the eyes that see what you see! ²⁴ For I tell you that many prophets and kings desired to see what you see, but did not see it, and to hear what you hear, but did not hear it."

The Disciples/Apostles – Luke 10:17-20

¹⁷ The seventy returned with joy, saying, "Lord, in your name even the demons submit to us!" ¹⁸ He said to them, "I watched Satan fall from heaven like a flash of lightning. ¹⁹ See, I have given you authority to tread on snakes and scorpions, and over all the power of the enemy; and nothing will hurt you. ²⁰ Nevertheless, do not rejoice at this, that the spirits submit to you, but rejoice that your names are written in heaven."

Angels Announcing the Savior's Birth – Luke 2:10-14

¹⁰ But the angel said to them, "Do not be afraid; for see—I am bringing you good news of great joy for all the people: ¹¹to you is born this day in the city of David a Savior, who is the Messiah, the Lord. ¹² This will be a sign for you: you will find a child wrapped in bands of cloth and lying in a manger." ¹³And suddenly there was with the angel a multitude of the heavenly host, praising God and saying, ¹⁴ "Glory to God in the highest heaven, and on earth peace among those whom he favors!"

John the Baptist – John 3:25-30

²⁵ Now a discussion about purification arose between John's disciples and a Jew. ²⁶ They came to John and said to him, "Rabbi, the one who was with you across the Jordan, to whom you testified, here he is baptizing, and all are going to him." ²⁷ John answered, "No one

can receive anything except what has been given from heaven. [28] You yourselves are my witnesses that I said, 'I am not the Messiah, but I have been sent ahead of him.' [29] He who has the bride is the bridegroom. The friend of the bridegroom, who stands and hears him, rejoices greatly at the bridegroom's voice. For this reason my joy has been fulfilled. [30] He must increase, but I must decrease."

The Early Church –Acts 8:4-8

[4] Now those who were scattered went from place to place, proclaiming the word. [5] Philip went down to the city of Samaria and proclaimed the Messiah to them. [6] The crowds with one accord listened eagerly to what was said by Philip, hearing and seeing the signs that he did, [7] for unclean spirits, crying with loud shrieks, came out of many who were possessed; and many others who were paralyzed or lame were cured. [8] So there was great joy in that city.

Acts 15:3

So they were sent on their way by the church, and as they passed through both Phoenicia and Samaria, they reported the conversion of the Gentiles, and brought great joy to all the believers.

In Heaven – Luke 15:3-10

[3] So he told them this parable: [4] "Which one of you, having a hundred sheep and losing one of them, does not leave the ninety-nine in the wilderness and go after the one that is lost until he finds it? [5] When he has found it, he lays it on his shoulders and rejoices. [6] And when he comes home, he calls together his friends and neighbors, saying to them, 'Rejoice with me, for I have found my sheep that was lost.' [7] Just so, I tell you,

there will be more joy in heaven over one sinner who repents than over ninety-nine righteous persons who need no repentance." 8 "Or what woman having ten silver coins, if she loses one of them, does not light a lamp, sweep the house, and search carefully until she finds it? 9 When she has found it, she calls together her friends and neighbors, saying, 'Rejoice with me, for I have found the coin that I had lost.' 10 Just so, I tell you, there is joy in the presence of the angels of God over one sinner who repents."

Our Churches and Communities

Without gospelizing, our worship of God becomes profane, hypocritical, and socially pacifying. The words of God's prophets clearly speak to this issue:

Isaiah

1 "Shout with the voice of a trumpet blast. Tell my people Israel of their sins! 2 Yet they act so pious! They come to the Temple every day and seem delighted to hear my laws. You would almost think this was a righteous nation that would never abandon its God. They love to make a show of coming to me and asking me to take action on their behalf. 3 'We have fasted before you!' they say. 'Why aren't you impressed? We have done much penance, and you don't even notice it!'

"I will tell you why! It's because you are living for yourselves even while you are fasting. You keep right on oppressing your workers. 4 What good is fasting when you keep on fighting and quarreling? This kind of fasting will never get you anywhere with me. 5 You humble yourselves by going through the motions of penance, bowing your heads like a blade of grass in the wind. You dress in sackcloth and cover yourselves with ashes. Is this what you call fasting? Do you really think this will please the LORD?

6 "No, the kind of fasting I want calls you to free those who are wrongly imprisoned and to stop oppressing those who work for you. Treat them fairly and give them what they earn. 7 I want you to share your food with the hungry and to welcome poor wanderers into your homes. Give clothes to those who need them, and do not hide from relatives who need your help.

8 "If you do these things, your salvation will come like the dawn. Yes, your healing will come quickly. Your godliness will lead you forward, and the glory of the LORD will protect you from behind. 9 Then when you call, the LORD will answer. 'Yes, I am here,' he will quickly reply.

"Stop oppressing the helpless and stop making false accusations and spreading vicious rumors! 10 Feed the hungry and help those in trouble. Then your light will shine out from the darkness, and the darkness around you will be as bright as day. 11 The LORD will guide you continually, watering your life when you are dry and keeping you healthy, too. You will be like a well-watered garden, like an ever-flowing spring. 12 Your children will rebuild the deserted ruins of your cities. Then you will be known as the people who rebuild their walls and cities.

13 "Keep the Sabbath day holy. Don't pursue your own interests on that day, but enjoy the Sabbath and speak of it with delight as the LORD's holy day. Honor the LORD in everything you do, and don't follow your own desires or talk idly. If you do this, 14 the LORD will be your delight. I will give you great honor and give you your full share of the inheritance I promised to Jacob, your ancestor. I, the LORD, have spoken!" (Isaiah 58:1-14, NLT)

Micah

6 What can we bring to the LORD to make up for what we've done? Should we bow before God with offerings

of yearling calves? 7 Should we offer him thousands of rams and tens of thousands of rivers of olive oil? Would that please the LORD? Should we sacrifice our firstborn children to pay for the sins of our souls? Would that make him glad? 8 No, O people, the LORD has already told you what is good, and this is what he requires: to do what is right, to love mercy, and to walk humbly with your God (Micah 6:6-8, NLT).

Amos

"21 I [the LORD] hate all your show and pretense — the hypocrisy of your religious festivals and solemn assemblies. 22 I will not accept your burnt offerings and grain offerings. I won't even notice all your choice peace offerings. 23 Away with your hymns of praise! They are only noise to my ears. I will not listen to your music, no matter how lovely it is. 24 Instead, I want to see a mighty flood of justice, a river of righteous living that will never run dry" (Amos 5:21-24, NLT).

Without gospelizing, worship loses its focus and meaning, drowning in the vacuum of a church that has become ingrown and as salt that has become savorless. In contrast, there is a spark and quickening in the worship of *Gospelizers*.

Genuine worship of the true and living God manifests itself in the congregation, as well as in the harvest-fields. A righteous and joyous worship experience both leads to and is the fruit of gospelizing (cf. Acts 13:2ff.).

Jubilee Gospelizing Worship

The **Fisk Jubilee Singers** come to mind.[167] Faced with impending financial collapse of Fisk University five years after its founding, the school's treasurer, George L. White, turned to a musical campaign to raise money. He organized the first itinerant Black religious singing group. These talented singers, after giving local concerts, set out on a Midwest trial tour in October 1871—in the period of Reconstruction. When these recently emancipated slaves added spirituals to the slave songs in their concerts, they achieved great success among the people. With jubilation they sang their way from the Midwest to the East, to Europe—gaining fame and raising $150,000 for their struggling university. By 1878 they had popularized and preserved the spirituals, touched the hearts of thousands in the harvest-fields, raised public awareness, and supported the cause of their institution and its people. In their own way the Fisk Jubilee Singers were Gospelizers. They fulfilled their "Jubilee" mission by joyfully worshiping and righteously serving God.

Contemporary **stepping and praise-dancing** are (or can become) the feet of gospelizing. We draw attention to the step dance team at the Junior High School in Springfield Gardens, Queens, New York.[168] As they perform their routines—improvisation, call and response, complex meters, propulsive rhythms and a percussive attack—they chant, "We are the children of righteousness." Church praise-dancers are just as vibrant—with their processions, bugles and drums, flags and banners, and belief in God. They have no necessary set style or technique. It's about worshiping God in a liturgical dance. Often it is jump and shout, old-time, foot-stomping religion. It is a witness.

Many diverse Christian young people are being attracted to steppin' and praise-dancin,' and both are done (or can be performed) in a "Gospel Spirit." They can also be done in a gospelizing spirit. Youth who gospelize may be the key to effectively changing our world. Charging and empowering our youth with a "Jubilee" gospelizing mission could be the turning point for alleviating the many terrorizing crises we face. (We have already discovered that properly educating young people is the most effective way to reverse the world's HIV/AIDS pandemic.) We must let our youth sacredly use what they know and like:

the art of music and dance. However, let us captivate their enthusiasm, harness their creativity, and focus their vision for gospelizing. Let us work with them to keep Christ as their center, the Church as their *Koinonia*, holistic gospelizing as their mission, the redemption of humanity as their righteous passion, and the worship and glory of God as the highest expression of their existence and being. Let us remember these words of Paul:

> [22] ...I have become all things to all people, that I might by all means save some. [23] I do it all for the sake of the gospel, so that I may share in its blessings (1 Corinthians 9:22b-23).

> [31] So, whether you eat or drink, or whatever you do, **do everything for the glory of God.** [32] Give no offense to Jews or to Greeks or to the church of God, [33] just as I try to please everyone in everything I do, not seeking my own advantage, but that of many, so that they may be saved. [11:1] Be imitators of me, as I am of Christ (1 Corinthians 10:31 – 11:1, emphasis mine).

And,

> And whatever you do, in word or deed, do everything in the name of the Lord Jesus, giving thanks to God the Father through him (Colossians 3:17).

Genuine and joyful worship springs from holistic dedication to Christ; from doing socially righteous and just work, showing compassion and care for people who are less fortunate, and in spreading the eternal riches of Jesus Christ and His Gospel (cf. Acts 8:4-8). Authentic gospelizing is worship, and praise-worthy.

"How beautiful are the feet of Gospelizers!"

(Romans 10:15b)

Appendix A

Occurrences of *Euangelizo* and *Euangelistes*

Following are the verses where *euangelizo* is found; translated in the NRSV.

Matthew 11:5 *the poor have good news brought to them*
Luke 1:19 [not in reference to Christ] *to bring you this good news*
Luke 2:10 *I am bringing you good news of great joy for all the people*
Luke 3:18 *he proclaimed the good news to the people*
Luke 4:18 *to bring good news to the poor*
Luke 4:43 *I must proclaim the good news of the kingdom of God*
Luke 7:22 *the poor have good news brought to them*
Luke 8:1 *bringing the good news of the kingdom of God*
Luke 9:6 *bringing the good news and curing diseases everywhere*
Luke 16:16 *the good news of the kingdom of God is proclaimed*
Luke 20:1 *telling the good news*
Acts 5:42 *they did cease to teach and proclaim Jesus as the Messiah*
Acts 8:4 *proclaiming the word*
Acts 8:12 *Philip, who was proclaiming the good news about the kingdom of God and the name of Jesus Christ*
Acts 8:25 *proclaiming the good news to many villages*
Acts 8:35 *he proclaimed to him the good news about Jesus*
Acts 8:40 *he proclaimed the good news to all the towns*
Acts 10:36 *preaching peace by Jesus Christ – he is Lord of all*
Acts 11:20 *proclaiming the Lord Jesus*
Acts 13:32 *we bring you the good news*
Acts 14:7 *and there they continued proclaiming the good news*
Acts 14:15 *and we bring you good news*
Acts 14:21 *After they had proclaimed the good news to that city*
Acts 15:35 *they taught and proclaimed the word of the Lord*
Acts 16:10 *God had called us to proclaim the good news to them*
Acts 17:18 *He seems to be a proclaimer of foreign divinities*
Romans 1:15 *hence my eagerness to proclaim the gospel to you*
Romans 10:15 *How beautiful are the feet of those who bring good news!*
Romans 15:20 *I make it my ambition to proclaim the good news*

1 Corinthians 1:17 *but to proclaim the gospel*

1 Corinthians 9:16 (twice) *If I proclaim the gospel....if I do not proclaim the gospel*

1 Corinthians 9:18 *that in my proclamation*

1 Corinthians 15:1 *the good news that I proclaimed to you*

1 Corinthians 15:2 *the message that I proclaimed to you*

2 Corinthians 10:16 *we may proclaim the good news in lands beyond you*

2 Corinthians 11:7 *I proclaimed God's good news to you free of charge*

Galatians 1:8 (twice) *proclaim to you a gospel contrary to what we proclaimed to you*

Galatians 1:9 *if anyone proclaims to you a gospel*

Galatians 1:11 *that the gospel that was proclaimed by me*

Galatians 1:16 *so that I might proclaim him among the Gentiles*

Galatians 1:23 *is now proclaiming the faith*

Galatians 4:13 *I first announced the gospel to you*

Ephesians 2:17 *So he came and proclaimed peace to you who were far off*

Ephesians 3:8 *grace was given to me to bring to the Gentiles the news*

1 Thessalonians 3:6 [not in reference to Christ] *the good news of your faith and love*

Hebrews 4:2 *the good news came to us just as to them*

Hebrews 4:6 *those who formerly received the good news*

1 Peter 1:12 *those who brought you good news by the Holy Spirit*

1 Peter 1:25 *that word is the good news that was announced to you*

1 Peter 4:6 *the gospel was proclaimed even to the dead*

Revelation 10:7 *as he announced to his servants the prophets*

Revelation 14:6 *with an eternal gospel to proclaim to those who live on the earth*

Following are the verses where *euangelistes* is found (NRSV).

Acts 21:8 *we went into the house of Philip the evangelist*

Ephesians 4:11 *that some would be apostles, some prophets, some evangelists, some pastors and teachers*

2 Timothy 4:5 *do the work of an evangelist*

Appendix B

Evangelism Imperatives and Approaches

"In six New Testament narratives we are charged specifically with the goal of world evangelization. These include Matthew 28:18-20, Mark 16:15-16, Luke 24:45-49, John 20:21-23, John 21:5-22 and Acts 1:4-8. By examining the words in each of these narratives, we can see the various aspects by which the world may be evangelized.

"**Receive!** the Holy Spirit. *labete.* This is a mandate for pneumatic evangelization, whose dominant characteristic is the outworking of the Holy Spirit. It is prayer evangelism, and involves renewal in the Spirit and intercession. For example, home churches in China have been known to meet for 24 hours and do nothing but pray for their fellow Chinese.

"**Go!** *poreuthentes.* This is a mandate for preparatory evangelism, whose dominant characteristic is 'sowing the seed.' This is 'pre-evangelism' in which Christian deeds help lay the groundwork for Christian witness. For example, many Christian relief agencies bring medical teams into countries for preventative health care, laying the groundwork for major evangelistic campaigns.

"**Witness!** *martyres.* This is a mandate for presence evangelism, whose dominant characteristic is its unorganized, private nature. It is personal, one-on-one evangelism. For example, many Middle Eastern Christians must be discreet, quiet witnesses for Christ, allowing their lives to demonstrate Christianity and choosing their moments of witness with care due to persecution.

"**Proclaim!** *keruxate.* This is a mandate for proclamation evangelism, whose dominant characteristic is its organized, public nature. This is preaching evangelism. It is best exemplified by large crusades....

"**Disciple!** *mathetesuate.* This is a mandate for persuasion evangelism, whose dominant characteristic is convert-oriented discipleship groups. This might also be called pressure evangelism, as it constantly puts the weight of apologetics, debate and discussion on those who would deny the Gospel. It can be seen in 'seeker's' groups, discipleship units and 'coffee houses' where the Gospel is discussed.

"**Baptize!** *baptizontes.* This is a mandate for [church-planting] evangelism, whose dominant characteristic is the planting of churches. This form of witness occurs when unbelievers witness churches being planted and Christianity growing.

"**Train!** *didaskontes.* This is a mandate for pedagogical evangelization, whose dominant characteristic is its orientation toward ministry. It might also be termed pastoral evangelism. For example, the presence of seminaries, open-air teaching, and theological training centers have an evangelistic effect."

From "The Scandal of World A," *World Evangelization Research Center,* (www.gem-werc.org/scandal/scandal.htm). This page is a subset of Global Diagram 6 in *World Christian Trends AD 30-AD 2200, Interpreting the Annual Christian Megacensus.* David Barrett and Todd Johnson. Pasadena: William Carey Library, 2001. Used by permission.

Abbreviations
(appearing mostly in Notes)

ABD	The Anchor Bible Dictionary
CEV	Contemporary English Version
Gk	Greek
HIV/AIDS	Human Immunodeficiency Virus/ Acquired Immune Deficiency Syndrome
ISBE	International Standard Bible Encyclopedia
IntlNT	Interlinear New Testament
KJV	King James Version
KJVSB	King James Version Study Bible
NIV	New International Version
NKJV	New King James Version
NLT	New Living Translation
NRSV	New Revised Standard Version
NBEA	National Black Evangelical Association
NICNT	The New International Commentary on the New Testament
TDNT	Theological Dictionary of the New Testament
UNAIDS	Joint United Nations Programme on HIV/AIDS
USAID	The US Agency for International Development
ZPEB	Zondervan Pictorial Encyclopedia of the Bible

Notes

---

[1] A search of similar translations of *euangelizo* in various literature has uncovered the following: *gospeled, gospeler, gospelers,
gospeling, gospelising, gospelism, gospelize, gospelized, gospelizer,
gospelizers, gospelizing, gospelled, gospeller, gospellere, gospellers,
gospelling.*

A. T. Robertson (*Word Pictures in the New Testament*)
translates the Greek term similarly *[gospelizer, gospelizing,
etc.]* at least sixteen times in fourteen passages. By far, his use
is the broadest, most insightful, and consistent. W. E. Vine
(*Collected Writings of W. E. Vine*) translates the term *gospeling* a
single time. *The MacArthur New Testament Commentary*
("Ephesians") translated *gospeled*. *The Biblical Illustrator* translates *gospelling* and *gospelising*. *The Wycliffe Bible Commentary*
uses the terms *gospelled* and *gospeling*. Martin Luther (com-
mentary on *Galatians*), and John Calvin each refers to
Gospellers. Interestingly, Lewis Bayly (d. 1631) wrote a work
("Practice of piety. Massachuset" [uniform title]) published in
Cambridge: "Printed for the Right Honorable Corperation in
London for the *Gospelizing* the Indins in New-England."
There are others.

See: *Word Pictures in the New Testament*, A. T. Robertson
(Nashville: Sunday School Board of the Southern Baptist
Convention, 1998); *Collected Writings of W. E. Vine* (Nashville:
Thomas Nelson Publishers, 1996); *The MacArthur N.T.C.*,
"Ephesians" (Chicago: Moody Press, 1987); The *Wycliffe Bible
Commentary, N.T.*, E. F. Harrison (Chicago: Moody Press,
1962); *The Biblical Illustrator*, Acts 16; *Luther's Commentary on
Galatians* (University of Wittenberg, 1535); *American Imprint
Collection*, John Eliot, abridged translation (Library of Con-
gress, 1685).

A general internet search uncovered a handful of uses.
"*Gospelizers*" was found in sermons/Bible studies on Acts 4:1-
12 ("the best route would be to put these 'gospelizers' in jail!"
"No Other Name,"); Acts 5:41-42 ("we are to be gospelizers;"
"Tell the Good News," Five-fold Vision Statements of Dr.
Barry - #3); Mark 16:14-18 ("Those who have believed are the
gospelizers of verse 15 and the gospelized of verse 16." "With

Signs Following," Louis Bartet); Romans 8:31-39 ("prosperity gospelizers;" "Comforting Questions"); and 1 Peter 1:1-24 (v. 12, "the gospelizers;" A. T. Robertson). Cf. also "gospelizing."

Our present treatment of the subject should not be confused with the turn-of-the-20th-century movement of "Social Gospelers/Gospelism." See, *A Dictionary of Biblical Tradition in English Literature*, David Lyle Jeffrey, s.v. "Millennium" (Wm. B. Eerdmans: Grand Rapids, 1997); "*A Dictionary of Christianity in America*, Daniel G. Reid, ed., s.v. "Social Gospel Movement," R. T. Handy (Downers Grove: InterVarsity Press, 1990); *On Being Witnesses*, J. J. Kritzinger, P. G. J. Meiring, W. A. Saayman (South Africa: Orion Publishers, Halfway House, 1994), 1:4.1.

2 See Job 38:1ff.; 40:6ff.

3 Composer Raymond Rasberry, copyright 1963.

4 Cf. the experience of Daniel when he saw his vision (Daniel 10:1-9ff.). John the apostle became dispirited when he saw the Lord (Revelation 1:12-17ff.) and Peter wept bitterly after having denied knowing Christ (Luke 22:54-62).

5 Romans 12:2 "Do not be conformed to this world, but be transformed by the renewing of your minds, so that you may discern what is the will of God — what is good and acceptable and perfect." [Or, *"what is the good and acceptable and perfect will of God."*]

6 For instance, several months prior to September 2001, while teaching a session on "Spiritual Gifts" at our church's Vacation Bible School, the Spirit of the Lord spontaneously spoke to me, prompting me to tell the class that based on an understanding of my spiritual gifts, I probably would not be pastoring the church for much longer. My abrupt announcement caught everyone including myself by surprise! Afterwards, the utterance went to "sleep" and was awakened by the Lord after September 11.

7 I "Recentered at the World Trade Center."

8 Cf. Charles E. Hummel *Tyranny of the Urgent* (Downers Grove: InterVarsity Press, 1994), rev. ed.

9 Recall the story of Martha and Mary. Luke 10:38-42 "38 Now as they went on their way, he [Jesus] entered a certain village, where a woman named Martha welcomed him into her

home. [39] She had a sister named Mary, who sat at the Lord's feet and listened to what he was saying. [40] But Martha was distracted by her many tasks; so she came to him and asked, 'Lord, do you not care that my sister has left me to do all the work by myself? Tell her then to help me.' [41] But the Lord answered her, 'Martha, Martha, you are worried and distracted by many things; [42] there is need of only one thing.[1] Mary has chosen the better part, which will not be taken away from her.'"[1] [Or, *"few things are necessary, or only one"* (an alternate reading).]

[10] Having contemplated taking a Sabbatical leave of one year from my pastorate, in order to immerse myself in the changes taking place in my life as directed by the Lord, and broaching the idea to the church, some dynamic circumstances emerged in the church family that dictated otherwise. For the good of the church and to avoid personal distraction, I resigned my pastorate and moved forward on my mission with a new freedom. I reassociated in fellowship with my home church.

[11] My wife and I made plans to liquidate certain assets in order to redistribute funds for our livelihood and to have resources to sow for the work of the Lord.

[12] The year 2002 marks a "Jubilee Year" in my life, and includes the 33rd anniversary of ministry in the Gospel of the Lord Jesus Christ; hence, my season of renewal.

[13] In October 2001, while attending a service at Stephen's COGIC in San Diego (pastored by Bishop George McKinney), a visiting minister spoke a word of prophecy for my life. He was very much unaware about the things the Lord was already speaking to me. The prophetic preacher said, "Don't retire, re-fire the furnace of your writing."

[14] Sometimes these services were God-directed and thus justified; on other occasions these good services proved only to become distractions, of which I had been undiscerning at the time. Ironically, sometimes the distraction came while working on writing projects that were not directly related to my primary thrust—producing Black Christian Biblical literature. Other sidetracks came with engaging myself in several managerial and operational type roles for worthy causes (e.g., serving on a neighborhood school council). But again, these

efforts were not my special calling. Neither were some well-intended entrepreneurial ventures. Hindsight helps to bring daily living into focus.

15 The faith community had turned anti-social behavior in on itself, and the Lord chose to use a people even more corrupt (the Chaldeans) to discipline and judge His covenant people. Habakkuk became "terrorized" at the thought of how the Lord would deal with the sin of His people. See Habakkuk 1:1ff.; 1:5ff.; 1:12ff.

16 I began *Gospelizers!*, I believe, in 1999. Approaching September 11, 2001 and thereafter, the subject became much clearer and more penetrating.

17 Several church groups, persuaded by Dr. Griffin's Biblical presentations, are in the process of following this teaching. Groups include several churches in India; the Chicago Baptist Institute; the American College of Theologians; the Pastor's Conference (Chicago); and his pastorate, First Baptist Congregational Church (Chicago).

18 Dr. Griffin provocatively challenges the time-commitment relationship of our churches to Christ with the question, "Dating or Marriage?" This is a fuller unpublished exposition addressing the Church's time-commitment-relationship with Christ. The work was prepared for use in the curriculum of the Chicago Baptist Institute, and included Scriptural documentation entitled "Vision for the New Millennium" (2000, 2002). Used by permission.

19 The authors of the book *On Being Witnesses* present a threefold formulation of mission, following the model of Gisbertus Voetius, a Dutch theologian. The immediate aim was "conversion;" the second aim, "planting of the church," was subordinate to the first; and the third aim, to which both first and second aims were subordinate, "the glory and manifestation of God's divine grace." Kritzinger, *Op. cit.*, 1.1.

With the understanding that the revelation of God given to humanity, including manifestations of His grace, is a by-product of His redemptive activity, it would seem that we cannot separate the salvation imperative from God's revelatory manifestation. God reveals Himself as the "I AM" to Moses in the process of redeeming the enslaved Hebrew-

Israelites from bondage (Exodus 3:13ff.). The same is true of the revelation of God's glory to Moses and the rest that God promises to grant to the people (Exodus 3:12-23). Thus, we cannot show or give witness to God's grace without simultaneously fulfilling a redemptive work among sinners — both proceed as a holiness call among saints.

Paul put the two together in Acts 20:24: "But I do not count my life of any value to myself, if only I may finish my course and the ministry that I received from the Lord Jesus, **to testify to the good news of God's grace**" (emphasis mine).

[20] "The work of reconciliation is both complete…and incomplete." The Gospel is "all that has been done in Christ for human redemption." Also, the Gospel is the offer freely extended to the hearers to "repent and believe the good news" by acceptance and obedience. R. P. Martin, *International Standard Bible Encyclopedia*, s.v. "Gospel," vol. 2, p. 532.

[21] Colossians 1:5b-6 "You have heard of this hope before in **the word of the truth, the gospel** [6] that has come to you. Just as it is bearing fruit and growing in the whole world, so it has been bearing fruit among yourselves from the day you heard it and truly comprehended **the grace of God**" (emphasis mine; cf. Galatians 2:5, 14). 1 Timothy 1:11 "…**the glorious gospel** of the blessed God" (emphasis mine).

[22] As of mid-2002, of the 6.2 billion persons in the world, there are 2 billion Christians, leaving 4.2 billion without Christ. Of those 4.2 billion, 1.6 billion of them are unevangelized; they have not yet been gospelized. This number represents 10,000 unreached people groups. "World A, the Unevangelized World," *World Evangelization Research Center: Pointing the Way to the Least Evangelized* (www.gem-werc.org/worlda .htm). Also, *U.S. Center for World Mission* (www.uscwm.org/ home.html).

[23] The Scripture warns sinners against disbelieving and disobeying God's *gospelizing*. "[1] Therefore, while the promise of entering his rest is still open, let us take care that none of you should seem to have failed to reach it. [2] For indeed the good news came to us [was *gospelized* to us] just as to them; but the message they heard did not benefit them, because they were **not united by faith** with those who listened. [6] Since

therefore it remains open for some to enter it, and those who formerly received the good news [who formerly were *gospelized*] failed to enter because of **disobedience**" (Hebrews 4:1-2, 6, emphasis mine).

[24] The thoughts of some will "accuse" them, while the thoughts of others will "excuse" them in the judgment. Cf. Romans 2:15.

[25] This is an often used phrase of Dr. Arthur D. Griffin. Cf. Hebrews 7:25 "Wherefore he is able also to save them to the uttermost that come unto God by him, seeing he ever liveth to make intercession for them" (KJV).

[26] "Presently, more than 70% of Christian effort and ministry is directed at people who already profess to be Christians, while less than 5% of our total missionary activity is focused on those who have never once had a chance to hear about the good news of the Gospel. This is a scandal." "World A, the Unevangelized World," *World Evangelization Research Center: Pointing the Way to the Least Evangelized, Op. cit.* Also, there are 10,000 unreached people groups. These are people groups which have "no indigenous community of believing Christians with adequate numbers and resources to finish evangelizing their community without further outside/cross-cultural assistance." *U.S. Center for World Mission, Op. cit.*

[27] Several approaches are suggested by various Scriptural terms for the believer's witness. Besides *"Gospelize!" (euangelizo)*, there is also:

"Receive!" (labete), "prayer evangelism"
"Go!" (poreuthentes), "preparatory evangelism"
"Witness!" (martyres), "presence evangelism"
"Proclaim!" (keruxate), "proclamation evangelism"
"Disciple!" (mathetesuate), "persuasion evangelism"
"Baptize!" (baptizontes), "[church-planting] evangelism"
"Train!" (didaskontes), "pedagogical evangelism"

An expanded list appears in Appendix B. Cf. "The Scandal of World A," *World Evangelization Research Center* (www.gem-werc.org/scandal/scandal.htm). (This is a subset of Global Diagram 6 in *World Christian Trends AD 30-AD 2200, Interpreting the Annual Christian Megacensus,* David Barrett and Todd Johnson. Pasadena: William Carey Library, 2001. Used by permission.)

[28] Cf. "*The Lausanne Covenant: '9. The Urgency of the Evangelistic Task,'"* (*U.S. Center for World Mission, Op. cit.*).

[29] The Gospel writer Luke uses the verb [*euangelizo; euangelizomai; "gospelizing"*] 25 times in Luke – Acts, to the almost complete exclusion of the noun [*euangelion; "Gospel"*]. "Luke deliberately avoided the noun since his purpose was to compose not a Gospel but a "life of Jesus" with **a paradigmatic value and related to the mission of the Church in Luke's day**" (emphasis mine) R. P. Martin, *ISBE*, s.v. "Gospel," vol. 2, p. 531.

[30] Refer to general survey of "Gospelizer" in note 1.

[31] "Uniformity in translation is difficult since no common English verb such as 'gospelize' is available to translate *euangelizo*. At times the immediate context also requires the verb to be translated in a way that does not permit uniformity (cf. Revelation 10:7)." "The terms 'good news,' 'gospel' (from Anglo-Saxon *god-spell*, which means 'good tidings'), Latin *evangelium*, and Gk, *euangelion* are literal equivalents. For the theological significance of these terms see *Gospel*." Stein, *ISBE*, vol. 2, p. 527. The English term "Gospel" originated before 950; ME *go(d)spell*, OE *godspell* (cf. GOOD, SPELL).

Euangelizo (and its forms) surface in 52 verses (appearing twice in two verses) in the N.T. text. The doublets are found in 1 Corinthians 9:16 and Galatians 1:8. The NRSV translates the term as *"proclaim,"* ("proclaims," "proclaiming," etc.); *"bring,"* etc.; and as *"announced," "telling," "preaching," "came,"* and *"received."* The term is always used to mean the Good News of Jesus Christ, the Son of God in all 54 appearances, except in Luke 1:19 and 1 Thessalonians 3:6, where it does not refer to Good News about Jesus.

[32] *Euangelistes*, "a bringer of good news." The English definition of evangelist is: "one who practices evangelism (the zealous preaching and dissemination of the gospel); especially a Protestant preacher or missionary." *The American Heritage Dictionary of the English Language*, New College ed., p. 453.

[33] "The gifts he gave were that some would be apostles, some prophets, some evangelists, some pastors and teachers…" (Ephesians 4:11). "The next day we left and came to

Caesarea; and we went into the house of Philip the evangelist, one of the seven, and stayed with him" (Acts 21:8). "What they said pleased the whole community, and they chose Stephen, a man full of faith and the Holy Spirit, together with Philip, Prochorus, Nicanor, Timon, Parmenas, and Nicolaus, a proselyte of Antioch"(Acts 6:5). "As for you, always be sober, endure suffering, do the work of an evangelist, carry out your ministry fully" (2 Timothy 4:5, cf. 1 Thessalonians 3:2, Philippians 2:22).

Sometimes evangelist/*gospelizer* is noted in exegetical treatments of especially Ephesians 4:11 in distinguishing the several gifts listed. Though there are only three so-named "evangelists" mentioned in the N.T., the not-so-named Gospelizers included many others, such as Euodia and Syntyche who "struggled beside me [Paul] in the work of the gospel" (cf. Philippians 4:3); a "famous" brother in the churches noted for "his proclaiming the good news" (cf. 2 Corinthians 8:18); and Epaphras who taught the Colossians (Colossians 1:5a-7; 4:12).

Of course, Jesus was a *Gospelizer*. John the Baptist was a *Gospelizer*. All the apostles were *Gospelizers*. Paul was a *Gospelizer*. Though used specifically of "the twelve" and Paul, in a wider sense "apostle" *(apostolos)* was used of other eminent Christian messengers. A study of *apostolos* in context in the following passages will confirm this use: Romans 16:7 (Andronicus and Junia); 1 Corinthians 4:6-9 (Apollos); Acts 14:1-4 (Barnabas); Philippians 2:25-30 (Epaphroditus); Galatians 1:19; 2:9 (James, the Lord's brother); (1 Thessalonians 1:1; 2:6; 2 Thessalonians 1:1 (Silas and Timothy); 2 Corinthians 8:16-24 (Titus). Study as well 2 Corinthians 8:18, 22, 23; and 1 Corinthians 15:7. By definition, all these believers must be regarded as *Gospelizers*. Cf. Herbert Lockyer, *All the Apostles of the Bible* (Grand Rapids: Zondervan Publishing House, 1972).

"But 'apostle' has general as well as specific meaning. An apostle is an envoy, sent on a mission to speak for the one sending him and having the sender's own authority. Although not numbered with *the* apostles, other believers in the early church were considered apostles—God's envoys, set apart for special ministry. These early apostles were itinerants, who [organized] and taught new churches much like modern missionaries. There is no indication in the NT that the office of apostle was an institutional one or a role to be filled in the local congregation. There is no indication that other envoys, sent by churches to their mission fields, had an authority similar to that of the Twelve or of Paul" (emphasis mine). Lawrence O. Richards, *Expository Dictionary of Bible Words* (Grand Rapids: Zondervan Publishing House, 1991), s.v. "Apostle."

[34] Furthermore, many believers excuse themselves from doing the work of an evangelist by appealing to the "gifted" nature of those so endowed. However, failure of any of Christ's followers to evangelistically spread the Word is never justified before God. Just as we believe in the "priesthood" of every believer, we must also accept what one writer prophetically refers to (based on Acts 8:1-4) as "the preacherhood" of all believers. He proceeds to say, "preachers and preaching" are both "conspicuously absent from the various lists of offices and gifts in the N.T....The call to preach...is the duty and privilege of every believer—for all who would not be ashamed of Jesus and his words (Mark 8:38)." *ISBE, Op. cit.*, vol. 3, p. 940f.

"Preaching," as used here, is not the formal delivering of sermons of which we are so accustomed. Rather, its use captures how preaching is viewed through the words and practices of the early church as revealed in the N.T. Scriptures. Originally and most often, it was a rather informal presentation of the Gospel message.

"The last fifty years have seen a growing scholarly consensus ...that 'preach' is somewhat infelicitous as a rendering for these two word groups [*kerysso* and *euangelizomai*]. 'Preach' accurately conveys the typically public and authoritative character of the various speech acts intended by these Greek terms; but it is a misleading translation to the extent that common English parlance uses 'preach' to refer to formal sermonizing directed to the faithful, while the NT uses both *kerysso* and *euangelizomai* to refer primarily (though not exclusively) to evangelistic activity directed to non-Christians." *ISBE, Op. cit.*, vol. 3, p. 941.

"Modes of communication do not always distinguish

preaching and teaching, and neither does audience. As to content, preaching without instruction lacks substance; teaching without *kerygma* lacks identity....Apart from a specific context, preaching is difficult to define. Even though preaching has long been significantly linked to the life and activity of both Jewish and Christian communities, it is so varied in content, mode, audience, and purpose that it resists the constraints of a dictionary, even a Bible dictionary." Fred B. Craddock, *The Anchor Bible Dictionary*, s.v. "Preaching," vol. 5, p. 453.

[35] For the phrasing, see: 1 Corinthians 15:1, "...*the gospel that I gospelized to you...*"; 2 Corinthians 11:7 "...*I gospelized God's gospel...*"; Galatians 1:11, "...*the gospel gospelized by me...*"; Revelation 14:6 "...*having an eternal gospel to gospelize...*" Both words, the "gospel" *(euangelion)* and *"gospelize" (euangelizo)*, appear in each phrase, intensifying the meaning.

[36] See Galatians 1:6-9 for the importance of adhering to the revealed content of the message.

As defined in a dictionary of English, "Gospel," as pertaining to our subject, is: "1) the teachings of Jesus and the apostles; the Christian revelation; 2) the story of Christ's life and teachings, especially as contained in the first four books of the New Testament, namely Matthew Mark, Luke, and John; 3) (usually capital) any of these four books; 4) glad tidings, especially concerning salvation and the kingdom of God as announced to the world by Christ." ["Gospel" may also mean, 1) something regarded as true and implicitly believed; 2) a doctrine regarded as of prime importance; 3) gospel music.] *Random House Dictionary of the English Language*, 2nd ed., unabridged, p. 824.

Cf. "evangel:" "1) the good tidings of the redemption of the world through Jesus Christ; the gospel; 2) any of the four Gospels; 3) doctrine taken as a guide or regarded as of prime importance; 4) good news or tidings."

Cf. "evangelical:" "1) pertaining to or in keeping with the gospel and its teachings; 2) belonging to or designating the Christian churches that emphasize the teachings and authority of the Scriptures, esp. of the New Testament, in opposition to the institutional authority of the church itself, and that stress as paramount the tenet that salvation is achieved by personal conversion to faith in the atonement of Christ; 3) designating Christians, esp. of the late 1970's, eschewing the designation of fundamentalist but holding to a conservative understanding of the Bible; 4) pertaining to certain movements in the Protestant churches in the 18th and 19th centuries that stress the importance of personal experience of guilt for sin, and of reconciliation of God through Christ; 5) marked by ardent or zealous enthusiasm for a cause; 6) an adherent to evangelical doctrines or a person who belongs to an evangelical church or party." *Ibid.*, p. 670.

37 "So he [Christ] came and proclaimed *[gospelized]* peace to you who were far off and peace to those who were near" (Ephesians 2:17).

38 "And the Word became flesh and lived among us, and we have seen his glory, the glory as of a Father's only son [or, *the Father's only son*], full of grace and truth" (John 1:14).

39 One author notes six themes in the passage: *death, resurrection, witness, Scripture, power (to change), and forgiveness.* ZPEB, s.v. "Gospel," vol. 2, p. 782.

40 An angel is "a messenger, especially of God;" and "a person who performs a mission of God or acts as if sent by God" *Random House Dictionary, Ibid.*, p. 79. Luke 2:10-11 "10 But the angel said to them, 'Do not be afraid; for see—I am bringing you good news *[gospelizing]* of great joy for all the people: 11 to you is born this day in the city of David a Savior, who is the Messiah, the Lord.'" Revelation 14:6 "Then I saw another angel flying in midheaven, with an eternal gospel to proclaim *[to gospelize]* to those who live on the earth—to every nation and tribe and language and people."

It has been suggested that the context of Revelation 14:6 implies an explanation of urgency, inasmuch as (out of the norm) an angel carries the salvation message. The mention of an angel in Revelation 14 is said to be the last such appearance, and thus there is no time to lose. An angel must take the message to all of humanity (or insure its delivery to all people on the earth). The eternalness of the Gospel highlights its "unity," "immutability," and its "permanent validity." Gerhard Kittle and Gerhard Friedrich, eds., *Theological*

Dictionary of the New Testament (Grand Rapids: Eerdmans Publishing, 1964), vol. 2, p. 735.

[41] The term *agathos* ("good things") is used alongside *euangelizo*, with the effect of re-emphasizing the goodness of the message/ministry. Cf. Isaiah 52:7 and Nahum 1:15.

[42] Mark 16:15 "And he said to them, 'Go into all the world and proclaim *[kerusso]* the good news to the whole creation.'"

[43] Mark 1:15 "[Jesus came]…saying, 'The time is fulfilled, and the kingdom of God has come near; repent, and believe in the good news.'"

[44] Romans 10:11 "The scripture says, 'No one who believes in him will be put to shame.'"

[45] Many Christians still picture missionaries as those who do their work outside the United States, or who dress in white, etc. Most often, the image of an evangelist in many of our minds evokes one who preaches (in contrast to also performing other good works) to win the lost to Christ. Being a disciple images one who, as a student, is learning to follow and live for Christ, and the witnessing activity of the learner may often become obscured in the background. To many of us, being a disciple is simply synonymous with being a Christian. The word apostle Biblically and primarily refers to one of "the Twelve" or to Paul, as especially chosen by Jesus. The word indicates a person who is (literally) "sent forth" into the mission-world by the Lord, and should be used accordingly. However, in our day, in many circles the term is endowed ecclesiastically with a high position in the Church, high authority.

[46] Cf. *pleraoo* "to render full, i.e., to complete."

[47] John 14:6 "Jesus said to him, 'I am *the way*, and the truth, and the life. No one comes to the Father except through me,'" (emphasis mine). Acts 9:2 "[Saul went to the high priest] and asked him for letters to the synagogues at Damascus, so that if he found any who belonged to *the Way*, men or women, he might bring them bound to Jerusalem" (emphasis mine). Acts 16:17 "While she [a slave girl] followed Paul and us, she would cry out, 'These men are slaves of the Most High God, who proclaim to you *a way* of salvation'" (emphasis mine). Acts 18:25, 26 "He had been instructed in *the Way* of the

Lord; and he spoke with burning enthusiasm and taught accurately the things concerning Jesus, though he knew only the baptism of John. He began to speak boldly in the synagogue; but when Priscilla and Aquila heard him, they took him aside and explained **the Way** of God to him more accurately" (emphasis mine). Acts 19:9 "When some stubbornly refused to believe and spoke evil of *the Way* before the congregation, he left them, taking the disciples with him, and argued daily in the lecture hall of Tyrannus" (emphasis mine). Acts 19:23 "About that time no little disturbance broke out concerning *the Way*" (emphasis mine). Acts 22:4 "I persecuted *this Way* up to the point of death by binding both men and women and putting them in prison" (emphasis mine). Acts 24:14 "But this I admit to you, that according to *the Way*, which they call a sect, I worship the God of our ancestors, believing everything laid down according to the law or written in the prophets" (emphasis mine). Acts 24:22 "But Felix, who was rather well informed about *the Way*, adjourned the hearing with the comment, 'When Lysias the tribune comes down, I will decide your case'" (emphasis mine).

48 Acts 11:26 "and when he [Barnabas] had found him, he brought him [Saul] to Antioch. So it was that for an entire year they met with the church and taught a great many people, and it was in Antioch that the disciples were first called *'Christians'*" (emphasis mine). Acts 26:28 "Agrippa said to Paul, 'Are you so quickly persuading me to become a *Christian?'*" (emphasis mine). 1 Peter 4:16 "Yet if any of you suffers as a *Christian*, do not consider it a disgrace, but glorify God because you bear this name" (emphasis mine).

49 Matthew 5:1-2 "1 When Jesus saw the crowds, he went up the mountain; and after he sat down, his *disciples* came to him. 2 Then he began to speak, and taught them…" (emphasis mine). Matthew 28:19 "Go therefore and make *disciples* of all nations, baptizing them in the name of the Father and of the Son and of the Holy Spirit" (emphasis mine).

50 Romans 1:7 "To all God's beloved in Rome, who are called to be *saints*: Grace to you and peace from God our Father and the Lord Jesus Christ" (emphasis mine). Romans 8:27 "And

God, who searches the heart, knows what is the mind of the Spirit, because the Spirit intercedes for the *saints* according to the will of God" (emphasis mine). Romans 16:1-2 "¹ I commend to you our sister Phoebe, a deacon of the church at Cenchreae, ² so that you may welcome her in the Lord as is fitting for the *saints*, and help her in whatever she may require from you, for she has been a benefactor of many and of myself as well" (emphasis mine). 1 Corinthians 1:2 "To the church of God that is in Corinth, to those who are sanctified in Christ Jesus, called to be *saints*, together with all those who in every place call on the name of our Lord Jesus Christ, both their Lord and ours" (emphasis mine).

51 Acts 5:14 "Yet more than ever *believers* were added to the Lord, great numbers of both men and women" (emphasis mine). 1 Timothy 4:12 "Let no one despise your youth, but set the *believers* an example in speech and conduct, in love, in faith, in purity" (emphasis mine).

52 Matthew 5:9 "Blessed are the peacemakers, for they will be called *children of God*" (emphasis mine). Luke 20:36 "Indeed they cannot die anymore, because they are like angels and are *children of God*, being children of the resurrection" (emphasis mine). John 1:12-13 "¹² But to all who received him, who believed in his name, he gave power to become *children of God*, ¹³ who were born, not of blood or of the will of the flesh or of the will of man, but of God" (emphasis mine). John 11:51-52 "⁵¹ He did not say this on his own, but being high priest that year he prophesied that Jesus was about to die for the nation, ⁵² and not for the nation only, but to gather into one the dispersed *children of God*" (emphasis mine). Romans 8:15-16 "¹⁵ For you did not receive a spirit of slavery to fall back into fear, but you have received a spirit of adoption. When we cry, *'Abba! Father!'* ¹⁶ it is that very Spirit bearing witness with our spirit that we are *children of God*" (emphasis mine). Galatians 3:25-26 "²⁵ But now that faith has come, we are no longer subject to a disciplinarian, ²⁶ for in Christ Jesus you are all *children of God* through faith" (emphasis mine). Philippians 2:15 "so that you may be blameless and innocent, *children of God* without blemish in the midst of a crooked and perverse generation, in which you

shine like stars in the world" (emphasis mine). 1 John 3:1-2
"¹ See what love the Father has given us, that we should be
called *children of God*; and that is what we are. The reason
the world does not know us is that it did not know him.
² Beloved, we are *God's children* now; what we will be has
not yet been revealed. What we do know is this: when he is
revealed, we will be like him, for we will see him as he is"
(emphasis mine). 1 John 3:10 "The *children of God* and the
children of the devil are revealed in this way: all who do not
do what is right are not from God, nor are those who do not
love their *brothers and sisters*" (emphasis mine). 1 John 5:2
"By this we know that we love the *children of God*, when we
love God and obey his commandments" (emphasis mine). 1
Timothy 5:1-2 "¹ Do not speak harshly to an older man, but
speak to him as to a *father*, to younger men as *brothers*, ² to
older women as *mothers*, to younger women as *sisters* — with
absolute purity" (emphasis mine).

53 Mark 10:43 "But it is not so among you; but whoever wishes to
become great among you must be your *servant [minister]*"
(emphasis mine). 2 Corinthians 6:4 "but as *servants [minis-
ters]* of God we have commended ourselves in every way:
through great endurance, in afflictions, hardships, calamities"
(emphasis mine). 1 Timothy 4:6 "If you put these instructions
before the brothers and sisters, you will be a good *servant
[minister]* of Christ Jesus, nourished on the words of the faith
and of the sound teaching that you have followed" (emphasis
mine).

54 Philippians 2:25 "Still, I think it necessary to send to you
Epaphroditus — my brother and co-worker and *fellow soldier*,
your messenger and minister to my need" (emphasis mine).
2 Timothy 2:3-4 "³ Share in suffering like a *good soldier* of
Christ Jesus. ⁴ No one serving in the army gets entangled in
everyday affairs; the *soldier's* aim is to please the enlisting of-
ficer" (emphasis mine). Philemon 2 "to Apphia our sister, to
Archippus our *fellow soldier*, and to the church in your
house" (emphasis mine). 2 Corinthians 10:3-5 "³ Indeed, we
live as human beings, but we do not *wage war* according to
human standards; ⁴ for the weapons of our *warfare* are not
merely human, but they have divine power to destroy

strongholds. We destroy arguments [5] and every proud obstacle raised up against the knowledge of God, and we take every thought captive to obey Christ" (emphasis mine).

[55] Luke 24:48 "You are *witnesses* of these things" (emphasis mine). Acts 1:8 "But you will receive power when the Holy Spirit has come upon you; and you will be my *witnesses* in Jerusalem, in all Judea and Samaria, and to the ends of the earth" (emphasis mine). 2 Timothy 2:2 "and what you have heard from me through many *witnesses* entrust to faithful people who will be able to teach others as well" (emphasis mine). Hebrews 12:1 "Therefore, since we are surrounded by so great a cloud of *witnesses*, let us lay aside every weight and the sin that clings so closely, and let us run with perseverance the race that is set before us" (emphasis mine). See also Acts 3:15; 5:32; 10:39, 41; 22:15, 20; 23:11; Revelation 2:13; 17:6.

[56] One writer affirms that there is no substantive difference between *euangelizo* and *kerusso*. "Related terms are the verb *kerysso*, 'preach,' and the noun *kerygma*, 'preaching,' both deriving from *keryx*, 'herald.' There is no apparent distinction in meaning between *euangelion* and *kerygma*." Martin, *Op. cit.*, p. 529. However, though not substantive, there are differences in their image-meaning, if not shades of difference in their application. "Although *euangelizomai* and *kerysso* have somewhat different nuances (*euangelizomai* usually emphasizing that it is the good news of divine salvation that is being preached), the two terms are often used synonymously to describe the authoritative proclamation of the divine message." G. P. Hugenberger, *ISBE*, s.v. "Preach," vol. 3, p. 940f.

Sometimes the two terms are used interchangeably in a specific context (cf. Romans 10:14-15). Also compare the parallel passages where *euangelizomai* is used in Luke 4:43 and 9:6, whereas *kerysso* is used in Mark 1:38 and 6:12. Also, Timothy was charged to "proclaim (*kerysso*) the message," and then to "do the work of an evangelist (*euangelistes*)" (2 Timothy 4:2, 5). Luke employs the terms side by side to capture the full mission of Jesus. "The 'preaching' [*kerysso*] and the 'proclaiming of the Gospel' [*euangelizo*] are not two separate things. The latter gives the content of the former.

'Whenever He [Jesus] proclaimed the evangel, He was preaching. Whenever He preached, He was proclaiming the evangel'" Norval Geldenhuys, *NICNT*, "Gospel of Luke" (Grand Rapids: Wm. B. Eerdmans Publishing Company, 1983), p. 239. The exegetical context helps decide the meaning.

The present exposition focuses on *euangelizo/euangelizomai*. *Euangelizomai* appears once in Matthew (11:5); ten times in Luke; fifteen times in Acts; 21 times in Paul's letters; two times in Hebrews; three times in 1 Peter; two times in Revelation; and does not appear in Mark, John's Gospel and the epistles, Ephesians, James, 2 Peter, or Jude. *TDNT, Op. cit.*, p. 717.

Our term appears intensively in the following passages: Acts 8, five times: vv. 4, 12, 15, 35, and 40; 1 Corinthians 9: vv. 16 (twice), and 18; Galatians 1, six times: vv. 8 (twice), 9, 11, 16, and 23; (also used in 4:13).

[57] Cf. Isaiah 52:7 and Nahum 1:15.

[58] Ephesians 1:13-14 "[13] In him you also, when you had heard the word of truth, the gospel of your salvation, and had believed in him, were marked with the seal of the promised Holy Spirit; [14] this is the pledge of our inheritance toward **redemption** as God's own people, to the praise of his glory" (emphasis mine).

[59] The sermon, "A Gospelizing Mission," was delivered during the Spring Revival Services in May 1999 at the First Baptist Congregational Church in Chicago; pastored by Dr. Arthur D. Griffin.

[60] *Euangelizesthai (gospelize)* is closely associated with complementary terms in: Acts 8:4-5 (*kerusso*, "proclaim"); Acts 5:42; 15:35 (*didasko*, "teach"); Acts 8:25; 11:19, 20 (*laleo*, "speak"); Acts 8:25 (*diamartureo*, "testify"); Acts 14:21 (*matheteuo*, "make disciples"); 1 Peter 1:12 (*angello*, "announce"). *TDNT, Op. cit.*, p. 720.

[61] See note 56.

[62] The key terms are *euangelizo* (an active verb; with its various morphological forms) and especially *euangelizomai* (middle voice), being much more common from classical times, and used more frequently than the active voice in the N.T. Both

verbs come from the same root, *angello* meaning to "announce," "proclaim," "publish news." These verb forms (and others) are used interchangeably throughout the study.

"Gospel" *(euangelion),* meaning "good news," is the content of what is preached. The activity is captured in the phrase "proclaim the good news" *(euangelizomai).* The "good" of the news comes from the prefix *eu* formed with the noun or the verb. The noun *angelos* means, "messenger; angel." *Euangelistes* is traditionally translated "evangelist."

"The noun form *'euangelion'* meant originally the reward offered to a messenger who brought news of victory in battle or escape from danger. By a natural transference it came to mean the content of the message he brought, i.e., not simply news but good news. The immediate reaction on receiving the good news was the offering of sacrifice to the gods as a token of gratitude." Martin, *Op. cit.,* p. 529. "In the N.T. period *'euangelizomai'* was the activity of public or private speaking, or else believing or receiving, but not writing or reading. Its use as applied to written documents (e.g., the Gospel of Luke) came at a later time (cf. Justin Martyr)." R. H. Stein, *ISBE,* s.v. "Good News; Preach Good News; etc.," vol. 2, p. 527. In addition, refer to various lexical aids, dictionaries, articles, and word studies. Reference may be made to "Gospel," "Evangelist," "Preach," "Good News," etc.

The progressive development of the idea in the author's mind first started from understanding the verb and thus the activity of *gospelizing,* and then proceeded to identifying as *Gospelizers* those who did the activity. In the course of study we were reminded of the noun translated as *evangelist,* and then came to appreciate fully one of its literal equivalents, "*Gospelizers,*" "a bringer of good news." The progression could also have gone from "Good News," to "Goodnewsing," to "Goodnewsers." These are also literal equivalents.

[63] Martin, *Op. cit.,* p. 530.

[64] Perhaps Jesus' actions are subtly conveyed as the KJV translates *euangelizo* as "...*showing the glad tidings,*" while the NKJV translates "*bringing the glad tidings,*" and the NRSV reads "*bringing the good news*"(emphasis mine).

A key passage in our understanding of *Gospelizers* is

Luke 4:16-21, which records the words of Jesus about Himself as the fulfillment of the Scripture, best understood in the context of the "Jubilee." His words are filled with verbs of action: "The Spirit of the Lord is upon me because he has anointed me to bring good news *[to gospelize]* to the poor. He has sent me to proclaim release to the captives and recovery of sight to the blind, to let the oppressed go free, and to proclaim the year of the Lord's favor" (vv. 18-19). Jesus was a *Gospelizer* in deed.

[65] "*Euangelizesthai* is not just speaking and preaching; it is proclamation with full authority and power. Signs and wonders accompany the evangelical message. They belong together, for the Word is powerful and effective. The proclamation of the age of grace, of the rule of God, creates a healthy sate in every respect...It is the powerful proclamation of the good news, the impartation of salvation." *TDNT, Op. cit.,* p. 720.

[66] Miracles are signs of the proclamation of the Word, a proclamation in which God is at work. Cf. *TDNT, Op. cit.,* p. 720.

[67] They may even be granted a share in the sufferings of the Gospel, and the power to endure those sufferings. Cf. 2 Timothy 1:8: "Do not be ashamed, then, of the testimony about our Lord or of me his prisoner, but join with me in suffering for the gospel, relying on the power of God." See also Philippians 1:29-30: "[29] For he has graciously granted you the privilege not only of believing in Christ, but of suffering for him as well — [30] since you are having the same struggle that you saw I had and now hear that I still have."

[68] An **effect** is "something brought about by a cause or agent; a result." The end result or accomplishment is in view. *Affect* means "to have an influence on; to bring about a change in." *The American Heritage Dictionary of the English Language,* New College ed., p. 415.

[69] Note that the women "provided for them out of their resources" (Luke 8:3). These were "gracious works."

[70] On *gospelizing* the kingdom and the Lordship of Christ, see Luke 16:16; Acts 10:36; and 11:20.

[71] Recall the relationship between *kerusso* and *euangelizo* explained in note 56.

[72] See note 56.

73 The Apostle Peter, during his *gospelizing* mission to the household of Cornelius, affirmed the *gospelizing* of God. "You know the message he sent to the people of Israel, preaching *[gospelizing]* peace by Jesus Christ—he is Lord of all" (Acts 10:36). See also Galatians 3:8, and Ephesians 2:14, 17. Christ came and "proclaimed *[gospelized]* peace" —a summary of Christ's total work.

74 Cross reference the following:

"grace"	John 1:16, 17; Acts 20:24
"power"	Romans 1:16; 1 Corinthians 1:17
	1 Thessalonians 1:5
"effectual working"	Ephesians 3:7
"good words"	Luke 4:22
"gracious works"	Matthew 5:16; Ephesians 2:10;
	Titus 3:8, 14; 1 Timothy 6:18
"perform"	Romans 4:21; Philippians 1:6
"working"	Mark 16:20; 1 Corinthians 12:10;
	Ephesians 1:19; 3:7; 4:16; Colossians 1:29;
	Hebrews 13:21
"great workings"	Acts 4:30; 5:12; 6:8; 15:12;
(wonders)	Ephesians 1:19; 1 Corinthians 12:10
"proclaiming"	Acts 16:10; 1 Corinthians 1:17;
	Galatians 1:9, 16
"performing"	Luke 13:32; John 9:16; 11:47
"impart" (share)	Romans 1:11; 1 Thessalonians 2:8
"announcing"	Galatians 4:13; 1 Peter 1:25
"living"	1 Corinthians 9:14; 2 Corinthians 13:5;
	Philippians 1:21
"manifesting"	John 2:11; 1 Corinthians 12:7; 1 John 3:8
"practicing"	Matthew 6:1; 23:3; 2 Corinthians 4:2;
	1 Timothy 4:15
"signing"	Mark 16:17, 20; John 6:2
"communication"	Ephesians 4:29; Colossians 3:8
"demonstration"	1 Corinthians 2:4
"transformation"	Romans 12:2; 2 Corinthians 3:18

75 Cf. Philippians 1:5 for "fellowship in the Gospel" (KJV); "sharing in the Gospel" (NRSV).

76 "Luke 8:1 gives us a comprehensive picture of the whole activity of Jesus. His whole life was proclamation of the

Gospel....His manifestation, not merely his preaching but his whole work, is described in terms of *euangelizesthai*. The context [of Ephesians 2:14-17] shows this." *TDNT, Op. cit.*, p. 718.

[77] See note 56.

[78] "The answer which Jesus gives to John the Baptist is that the longed for time is now dawning, that the eschatological good news expected from the days of Isaiah is now being proclaimed, and that the word has power and brings into effect what is spoken. Word and miracle, the proclamation of the glad tidings and the resurrection of the dead are signs of the Messianic age." *TDNT, Op. cit.*, p. 718.

[79] See note 56.

[80] See note 56.

[81] See note 56.

[82] See note 56.

[83] Jesus was "...teaching the people in the temple and telling the good news [*gospelizing*]..." (Luke 20:1). Notice that the chief priests, scribes, and elders asked Jesus, "[B]y what authority are you doing these things?" (cf. Luke 20:1ff.). As Matthew 21:14 indicates, Christ's authority was not just in speaking, and teaching, but also in acting and performing miracles.

[84] John 5:35 "He [John the Baptist] was a burning and shining lamp, and you were willing to rejoice for a while in his light."

[85] See note 56.

[86] Key verses in Acts 5 are: v. 12 (signs and wonders); v. 15 (sick); v. 16 (sick and demon-tormented, cured); v. 20 (tell the people the whole message); v. 25 (teaching the people); v. 28 (not to teach in this name); v. 40 (not to speak in the name of Jesus); v. 42 (to teach and proclaim [*gospelize*] Jesus as the Messiah.

[87] See note 56.

[88] Notice the synonymous nature of *gospelizing* with "the word," "the kingdom of God," and "the name of Jesus Christ" in Acts 8:4 and 12. Cf. Acts 8:35, "...he [Philip] proclaimed to him [the Ethiopian] the good news [*gospelized* to him] about Jesus."

[89] In Philippians 1:12-18 Paul expressed joy and rejoicing that *gospelizing* was taking place in the city of his imprisonment, despite the motives of the messengers.

[90] The underlying Greek verb is *euangelizo/euangelizomai*. Its meaning is explained in note 60 and 62..

[91] "Signs," "cures," "great miracles," "unclean spirits...come out," (exorcisms), etc. See Acts 8:6, 7, 13. "Wonders," "healings," "grace," and "fillings" of the Spirit, etc. are additional examples of miraculous outcomes. Study Acts 2:43; 3:7, 16; 4:9-10, 22, 30, 31; 5:12; 6:8; 8:6-7, 13; 14:3-4, 9-10; 15:12; 19:11-12.

[92] Luke 4:16-22, 40; 8:2, 21; 20:1-2.

[93] "As a result of persecution in Jerusalem the Gospel is taken further afield." B. Friedrich. *TDNT*, s.v. *"euangelizomai, euangelion, proeuangelizomai, euangelistes,"* p. 719.

[94] See *9.11.01: African American Leaders Respond to an American Tragedy,* Martha Simmons and Frank A Thomas, eds.; (Valley Forge: Judson Press, 2001).

9.11.01 offers a cross-section of responses by leaders to the September 11, 2001 terrorist attacks. Most of these responses were initially sermons from the African American pulpit. They reflect the mindset and emotions of prophetic preachers in the "moments" (days) immediately following the attacks. Most of these messages, though spoken to local church audiences, were appeals made to the nation, and called for change of one sort of another. Others directed their exhortations more to believers and the Church community at large. Many of these responses were multi-faceted. These Black Christian messages "encompass but also eclipse" matters of race (Martha Simmons, p. x.). They are presented under four headings: *Preach, Prophesy, Persevere,* and *Proclaim,* and each message has its own title.

We should keep in mind that these responses were immediate in nature, and thus, in some cases, were more general rather than strategic in tone. They were visceral, and demonstrate a great depth of spirituality, honesty, and courage of outspoken Christian leadership in a time of national crisis. The collection is valuable.

I note the following observations of these varied responses to terrorism, as they are indicative of shared sentiments and relate to the mission of Gospelizers. Several specific responses carried a definite gospelizing tone. In general, the responses emphasized:

- The racial terrorism experienced by Africans in America (Martha Simmons, p. xi., T. D. Jakes, p. 30; Walter S. Thomas, p. 38; Charles E. Booth, p. 51; Calvin O. Butts III, 100; Richard W. Willis, Sr., p. 166).
- Managing the fear caused by terror (Calvin O. Butts III, p. 99).
- Attending to global responsibilities (Robert M. Franklin, p. 80).
- It's time for the nation "…to opt back in…" to "…the obligations of public citizenry" (Gail E. Bowman, p. 9).
- Advocating reconciliation: "Beyond retaliation we must think of reconciliation.…Why are we so hated around the world?" (Gardner C. Taylor, pp. 34, 35) "…[T]he advocates of reconciliation will have to remain as committed to building a global community as the advocates of violence are to tearing it down" (Richard W. Willis, Sr., p. 167).
- Focusing the Church on helping the marginalized masses of people in prisons, detention centers and mental hospitals, as well as the homeless on the streets of America. "Where is there a higher challenge and call to witness from the church?" (Cain Hope Felder, p. 16)
- Caring for Africa and the AIDS situation: "Come to the crumbling cities of the world, to impoverished nations where AIDS and war, sickness and poverty, capitalistic globalization, pain and revenge, all ravage the whole continent of Africa…" (Charles G. Adams, p. 144).
- Understanding the angst of the world's poor against our nation (Jesse Jackson, Sr., p. 111).
- Criticizing the worship of materialism; that is "…having an uncritical celebration of goods and services and materials of life, while the masses go down the drain" (Michael Eric Dyson, pp. 73, 75).
- Declaring war on greed, AIDS, an inadequate health-care system, and other problems (Jeremiah A. Wright, Jr., pp. 88, 90).
- The insensitivity of the U.S. walking out on the UN Conference on racism and xenophobia (William D.

Watley, p. 135; Michael Eric Dyson, p. 67; Robert M. Franklin, p. 80).

- The need to reprioritize: "This is a good time to take inventory. In the wake of September 11, 2001 we need to reaccess our values, reestablish our priorities, and scrutinize our relationship with Jesus Christ" (Vashti Murphy McKenzie, p. 121; Jeremiah A. Wright, Jr., p. 88).

- Answering the missionary call to go to Africa to preach the Gospel of Jesus Christ (Delores Carpenter, p. 62).

- The mandate to proclaim the Gospel: "The pulpit has the same mandate it has in time of peace — that is to preach the gospel of our Lord and Savior Jesus Christ" (Carolyn Ann Knight, p. 120).

- The salvation and efficacy of Jesus: "There is salvation only in the love of Jesus Christ..." (Peter J. Gomes, p. 154). "...[W]e pray in the name of Jesus Christ..." (J. Alfred Smith, Jr., p. 169).

- The victory of Christ's resurrection over terror: "...[T]he resurrection is the guarantor that evil will not win..." (Frank A. Thomas, p. 174).

[95] The MAAFA is a Kiswahili term for "disaster" or "terrible occurrence." This African word best describes the more than 500 years of suffering among people of African descent due to slavery, imperialism, colonialism, invasions and exploitation.

[96] Facts/projections reported at "AIDS/HIV in the Black World," Consultation, Action, and Coalition Pre-convention of the National Black Evangelical Association (NBEA), March 13-16, 2002, San Diego, CA. For information on the coalition, contact: NBEA, P. O. Box 4311, Chicago, IL 60680. (E-mail: nbeachicago@aol.com.)

HIV stands for Human Immunodeficiency Virus. AIDS is Acquired Immune Deficiency Syndrome. HIV causes AIDS.

See also: World Relief (www.worldrelief.org/what_we _do/aids_ministries/continent_in_crisis.asp); UNAIDS Report, AIDS Epidemic Update, July 2002, December 2001; UNAIDS: AIDS Epidemic Update, December, 2000; UNAIDS: Report on the global HIV/AIDS Epidemic, June 2000; UNAIDS Fact Sheet: AIDS in Africa, Johannesburg, 30th

November 1998; (www.avert.org/aidsinafrica.htm); USAID (www.usaid.gov).

[97] Thank the Lord for United Nations Secretary General Kofi Annan for bringing AIDS to the forefront of international attention in a U.N. special session on the disease in June 2001.

[98] In July 2002 at the session of the U.N. Economic and Social Council, the Joint United Nations Programme on HIV/AIDS (UNAIDS) released a new report on the AIDS pandemic. The press release, joined by the United Nations International Children's Emergency Fund (UNICEF) and the World Health Organization (WHO), was released prior to the 14th International Conference on AIDS, held in Barcelona, Spain. Findings of the report detail the following:

• The AIDS/HIV pandemic among the worst affected countries has not leveled off, as had been expected, but in fact is spreading rapidly into new populations in Africa, Asia, the Caribbean, and Eastern Europe; the pandemic is still in its early stages;

• By 2020, 68 million persons are expected to die from AIDS in the 45 most affected countries, if expanded prevention and treatment efforts do not occur;

• AIDS is spreading through heterosexual contact at an accelerated rate in places where the epidemic seemed stable — China, Indonesia, the Russian Federation, Eastern Europe, and parts of Western and Central Africa;

• HIV/AIDS is spreading rapidly among teens and young adults, and especially in among females; ages 17-24 are at the greatest risk, and are becoming infected at the rate of 6,000 each day; at the epidemic's peak in South Africa, there will be 17 as many deaths among persons 17-34 than there would have been without AIDS;

• The vast majority of the world's young people "have no idea" how HIV/AIDS is transmitted or how to protect themselves from the disease; in sub-Saharan Africa more than two-thirds of newly-infected 15-19 year olds are female;

• In 2001, less than 4% of persons needing access to antiretroviral treatment for HIV in the developing world received the medicine; in Africa only 30,000 of the 28.5 million infected persons received antiretroviral therapy; AIDS killed 2.2 million in Africa;

- Over 28 million Africans are living today with HIV; in some countries over 30% of the adult population are infected; nearly 40% in Botswana;
- Besides HIV/AIDS, tuberculosis and malaria are also killing millions each year;
- By the end of 2002, 3 billion dollars will have been given to fight the HIV/AIDS pandemic; $10 billion is what is actually needed among low- and middle-income countries to adequately combat the disease.

(See: www.unaids.)

[99] "HIV infection among U.S. women has increased significantly over the last decade, especially in communities of color. The U.S. Centers for Disease Control and Prevention (CDC) estimates that, in the United States, between 120,000 and 160,000 adult and adolescent females are living with HIV infection, including those with AIDS." See: "The Body: Body Positive—At Risk: Young, Minority, and Lesbian Women." *The Body Positive Magazine*, January/February 2002. (www.thebody.com/bp/janfeb02/women_risk.lhtml). Also, "The Body: AIDS Action—Policy Facts: Women and HIV/AIDS." See also, "The Women's Interagency HIV Study," *Epidemiology*, March 1998, Vol. 9, No. 2, p. 117-125.

The New York Times has reported that 850,000-950,000 Americans are infected with HIV. Of these, 180,000-280,000 have the virus but do not know it (February 26, 2002).

[100] Stated by the Rev. Dr. Myers, June 2002 in a personal interview. Bangladesh is on the border between India and Burma. At the time Humphreys County had the highest infant mortality rate in Mississippi, and Mississippi had the highest rate in the country.

Dr. Myers is co-founder with Sylvia Holmes-Myers of the Myers Foundation for Indigent Health Care and Community Development (1990). Their foundation is a gospelizing ministry in its essence, for it is established to **"demonstrate the Gospel of Jesus Christ through holistic ministry to the poor in rural America."**

Dr Myers also heads the National Juneteenth Christian

Leadership Council, a major promoter of the African-American holiday. See: www.myersfoundation.net.

[101] Jacob Levenson, "On the Road in Third-World Alabama," *Oxford American Magazine,* Fall 2001, p. 36-46.

[102] There were about 34.3 million persons living with AIDS at the end of 1999. Three million died from AIDS in 2001.

[103] A major lobbying effort pre-September 11, 2001 generated only $200 million from the U.S. government for an international fund to fight the pandemic/epidemics. *In Focus,* the organizational newsletter of Project Inform, did a splendid article (no. 114, March 2002) showing the similarities and dissimilarities of the terrorism of September 11, and the terrorism of AIDS, both in the nature and impact of the devastations, as well as in the response of individuals and the nation to the terrorism of each experience. In 2002 contributing countries gave only three billion dollars to the AIDS/HIV pandemic worldwide. (Cf. the UNAIDS report released in July 2002.)

[104] According to an article by Tonya Adams in the January/February 2002 *CRISIS Magazine,* Black churches are beginning to take the lead in AIDS outreach. They are supplying more than spiritual guidance. They also offer services ranging from counseling and HIV testing, to helping people cover bills.

Also, the Church must raise a spiritual and moral voice against the unrighteous actions of multi-national pharmaceutical companies that impede progress in solving the AIDS crisis, estimated as 40 million infected persons worldwide. These conglomerates use very ungodly strategies by fighting against accessibility to generic antiretroviral "cocktails" that prolong the health and life of AIDS patients, and maintaining high/unaffordable costs for life-saving drugs. Cf. Article by Christ Casacchia on Tina Rosenberg, "Medill Grad/Pulitzer Winner Rosenberg Lectures at NU on AIDS Crisis," *Evanston Express,* February 10-16, 2002, p. 4.

[105] 2 Timothy 3:1 "You must understand this, that in **the last days distressing times** will come" (emphasis mine). 2 Timothy 4:1-2 "In the presence of God and of Christ Jesus, who is to judge the living and the dead, and in view of his appearing

and his kingdom, I solemnly urge you: proclaim the message; be persistent whether the time is favorable or **unfavorable**; convince, rebuke, and encourage, with the utmost patience in teaching" (emphasis mine). 1 Corinthians 7:29-31 "I mean, brothers and sisters, **the appointed time has grown short**; from now on, let even those who have wives be as though they had none, and those who mourn as though they were not mourning, and those who rejoice as though they were not rejoicing, and those who buy as though they had no possessions, and those who deal with the world as though they had no dealings with it. For the present form of this world is passing away"(emphasis mine). Romans 13:11-14 "Besides this, you know what time it is, how it is now the moment for you to wake from sleep. For salvation is nearer to us now than when we became believers; **the night is far gone**, the day is near. Let us then lay aside the works of darkness and put on the armor of light; let us live honorably as in the day, not in reveling and drunkenness, not in debauchery and licentiousness, not in quarreling and jealousy. Instead, put on the Lord Jesus Christ, and make no provision for the flesh, to gratify its desires" (emphasis mine).

[106] Romans 13:12a "the night is far gone, the day is near."

[107] Note the emphasis of the Scriptural context and content on money and riches: Luke 16:1-13, about riches; 16:14-15, lovers of money; 16:18, adultery; and 16:19-31, a rich man and Lazarus.

At first glance, Jesus' words about marriage and adultery (16:18) may appear to be unrelated to the money/riches theme. However, these words are a sharp rebuke against men treating women as objects and playthings. Men were marrying women just to sexually exploit them. When the men became tired of the relationship they would release themselves of any financial obligations or burdens associated with maintaining the marriage by divorcing and dumping their wives cold, leaving them only to be exploited once again by the next man in line. Hence, by their cruel and heartless dominating male practices, these men were sinfully violating God's institution of marriage and made themselves adulterers and breakers of God's divine law. They substituted sex for the sacredness of relationship, and valued material wealth over loving a wife. The Gospel of Jesus condemned these men and their materialistic values.

108 See the context of persecution against believers of Matthew 24:14: "And this good news of the kingdom will be proclaimed throughout the world, as a testimony to all the nations; and then the end will come" (cf. 24:9ff.).

109 Paul's gospelizing to the Galatians was marked by an impartation of the Spirit and miracles. Cf. Galatians 3:5: "Well then, does God supply you with the Spirit and work miracles among you by your doing the works of the law, or by your believing what you heard?"

110 See James D. G. Dunn, *Word Biblical Commentary, vol. 38b: Romans 9-16* (Dallas: Word Books, 1998).

111 Pathetically, some of our churches are little more than "centers of entertainment and commerce." (A verbal critique by Rev. Dr. Cain Hope Felder of Howard University, at an Urban Outreach meeting in Chicago, February, 2002.)

112 Warriors.

113 Some mission-minded individuals and organizations would say "peoples" or "people groups." A "people group" is "A significantly large ethnic or sociological grouping of individuals who perceive themselves to have a common affinity for one another. For evangelistic purposes it is the largest group within which the Gospel can spread as a church planting movement without encountering barriers of understanding or acceptance." Unreached People (sometimes called "Hidden Peoples") are "a people group which has no indigenous community of believing Christians with adequate numbers and resources to finish evangelizing their community without further outside/cross-cultural assistance." "The terms and definitions used above are commonly referred to as the 'consensus definitions.' These were the result of a meeting held in Chicago in March of 1982 at which most of the mission agencies working among unreached peoples were represented" (U.S. Center for World Mission, Pasadena, CA; www.adopt-a-people.com).

114 Ephesians 5:23b "…Christ is the head of the church, the body of which he is the Savior."

[115] 2 Timothy 4:7c Paul said, "...I have kept the faith [the trust]." He told Timothy, "...I charge you to keep the commandment without spot or blame until the manifestation of our Lord Jesus Christ" (1 Timothy 6:13c-14).

[116] The "nation" *(ethnos)* contextualization of the Gospel by *Gospelizers* serves to keep their witness in focus. It does not prohibit cross-cultural *gospelizing*, and does not produce churches of a "homogenous members only" nature. These are grave transgressions: a violation of God's matchless grace; apartheid (and anathema!) in the Church, Christ's Body; and a stumbling block to the salvation of sinners. Some institutions of society (even some Christian ones) must of nature and necessity be exclusive; the Church never! The Church is an open-ended fellowship. "Whosoever will, let him come!"

[117] See note 56.

[118] A truth Hilliard has cogently taught on many different occasions.

[119] See *TDNT*, and other word studies. Cf. Acts 2:42; 1 Corinthians 1:9; 10:16; 2 Corinthians 6:14; Philippians 1:5; 2:1; 1 John 1:3.

[120] The earliest believers were committed to "the Way" of the Lord even before they were called "Christians." Cf. Acts 9:2; 11:26.

[121] Gk. *mathetes* "learner, pupil, disciple."

[122] Cf. 1 John 5:1-2 "[1] Everyone who believes that Jesus is the Christ has been born of God, and everyone who loves the parent loves the child. [2] By this we know that we love the children of God, when we love God and obey his commandments."

[123] "The call to conversion should be a call to service....putting ourselves at [God's] disposal, as workers in his vineyard....The person who reacts positively to the call to conversion thereby accepts the responsibility and privilege of becoming an evangelist calling others to conversion." Kritzinger, *Op. cit.*, section 1.4.2.5.

[124] For some reason or another, the apostles didn't leave Jerusalem. The irony of Acts 8:1 is revealing: "all except the apostles" — except those who were (literally) "sent forth"! *(apostello)* — were scattered and went proclaiming.

[125] "World evangelization requires the whole Church to take the whole gospel to the whole world." "The Lausanne Covenant: '6. The Church and Evangelism.'" *Ibid.*

126 See note 56.

127 Luke 6:12-16.

128 Cf. Acts 13:1-4.

129 A good point is made: "Usually the theorizing and formulation in mission is done afterwards. The action comes first. Mission is as old as the church, but very little Missiology (a systematic study of mission) was done before the 19th century. It was only after many years of practical mission, and with certain traditions already established, that mission leaders came to the point of formulating policy ideas. It was not often that a pioneer mission enterprise started with a clear policy and theory in place." Kritzinger, *Op. cit.*, section 4:7. In other words, as led by the Spirit, act on what you know now; evaluate what was done later.

130 This is the "incarnational" approach, which "identifies" and "bonds" with people. Cf. Kritzinger, *Op. cit.*, 4:2.3.

131 Matthew 25:40 "And the king [Jesus] will answer them, 'Truly I tell you, just as you did it to one of **the least** of these who are members of my family, you did it to me'" (emphasis mine). The "least" were the hungry, thirsty, strangers, those without clothes, the sick, and prisoners. The "lost" are those without salvation (Luke 19:10). The "unwell" are those who are afflicted in body or mind, or those in need of repentance. "Jesus answered, 'Those who are well have no need of a physician, but those who are sick; I have come to call not the righteous but sinners to repentance'" (Luke 5:31-32).

132 In the story of Jesus and Zacchaeus there is a relationship between the "lost," the "poor," and the "salvation" brought by Jesus to the community. Luke 19:8-10 "Zacchaeus stood there and said to the Lord, 'Look, half of my possessions, Lord, I will give to the **poor**; and if I have defrauded anyone of anything, I will pay back four times as much.' Then Jesus said to him, 'Today **salvation** has come to this house, because he too is a son of Abraham. For the Son of Man came to seek out and to save the **lost**'" (emphasis mine).

133 In 1998, I preached a series of messages in Chicago at Greater Union Baptist Church (my former pastorate), and at revival services at Austin Corinthian Baptist Church (Pastor, Clarence L. Hilliard). Since then similar messages have been

preached at other churches and meetings elsewhere. Recently published books are *The Holy Bible: The African American Jubilee Edition* (New York: The American Bible Society, 1999), and *The Holy Bible: The Jubilee Legacy Bible* (Nashville: Townsend Press, 1999).

[134] World Relief reports that "AIDS is devastating Africa. Claiming more than 6,500 lives every day, this incurable disease is killing 2.4 million Africans a year—leaving children without parents and communities in despair. The AIDS numbers are staggering—especially in Africa's poorest countries in the central, eastern and southern regions of this vast continent. In some nations, as many as one-in-three adults carry the HIV virus that causes AIDS." World Relief, *Op. cit.*

"Africa continues to dwarf the rest of the world in how the region has been affected by AIDS. Africa is home to 70% of the adults and 80% of the children living with HIV in the world. The estimated number of newly infected adults and children in Africa reached 3.4 million at the end of 2001. It has also been estimated that 28.1 million adults and children were living with HIV/AIDS in Africa by the end of the year. AIDS deaths totaled 3 million globally in 2001, and of the global total 2.3 million AIDS deaths occurred in Africa." Avert, *Op. cit.*

[135] The socio-economic aftermath is a devastating crisis in the areas of health, education, industry, agriculture, transportation, human resources, defense, and the overall economy.

[136] See the author's *The Black Presence in the Bible, The Black Presence in the Bible and the Table of Nations,* and *Black Biblical Studies, An Anthology of Charles B. Copher: Biblical and Theological Issues on the Black Presence in the Bible* (Chicago: Black Light Fellowship, 1990, 1993). See also: www.blacklightfellowship.com. There are other works and study Bibles on the subject.

[137] I shared about Blacks in the Bible with several groups at the Wycliffe headquarters in Orlando, Florida in February 2002. The majority of white mission workers in attendance responded very positively to the presentation. This Biblical truth is very important for spreading the Gospel among Africans and other people of color in our world.

138 The authors of *On Being Witnesses* address "the comprehensive approach" that embraces five categories: *kerygma* (proclamation)/*euangelizo* (evangelism); *diakonia* (ministry of service); *koinonia* (communion or fellowship); *leitourgia* (the public worship service of God); and *dikaioma* (justice). Under these five areas, they believe "the total missionary work of the church can be accommodated." Kritzinger, *Op. cit.*, 1:5; 4:4; and 4:6.3.

139 Cf. *On Being Witnesses*, models of evangelism and service, Kritzinger, *Op. cit.*, 4.

140 See note 56.

141 On the growth of early churches see Acts 9:31; 14:23; 15:40-41; 16:4-5; Romans 16:1, 4-5, 16.

142 Acts 1:1-2, 8 "¹ In the first book, Theophilus, I wrote about all that Jesus did and taught from the beginning ² until the day when he was taken up to heaven, after giving instructions through the Holy Spirit to the apostles whom he had chosen. ⁸ 'But you will receive power when the Holy Spirit has come upon you; and you will be my witnesses in Jerusalem, in all Judea and Samaria, and to the ends of the earth.'"

143 In 2 Corinthians 8:18, "proclaiming the good news," is parallel to "among all the churches."

144 Matthew 13:31-33 "³¹ He put before them another parable: 'The kingdom of heaven is like a mustard seed that someone took and sowed in his field; ³² it is the smallest of all the seeds, but when it has grown it is the greatest of shrubs and becomes a tree, so that the birds of the air come and make nests in its branches.' ³³ He told them another parable: 'The kingdom of heaven is like yeast that a woman took and mixed in with three measures of flour until all of it was leavened.'"

145 The Black presence in the church at Antioch is quite evident to some. Consider: Paul resembled an Egyptian enough to be mistaken as an Egyptian revolutionary (Acts 21:38). Barnabas was a native of Cyprus and a Levite, implying genealogy and geographical African ancestry (Acts 4:36). Simeon was called "Niger," signifying his nationality/color as "the black man." Lucius, a Hamite, was from Cyrene, in Cyranaica, North Africa (present-day Libya). And Manaen was the "foster brother" of Herod the ruler. Perhaps implying a shared identity with the

Notes 207

Herodians, who were identifiably Black as traceable through the explicitly Hamite Canaanite wives of Esau, the Edomites, and the Idumeans from which sprang the Herodians. At any rate, these Antiochan prophets and teachers were ethnically diverse, and definitely led by the Spirit of God.

146 "(Already) called," a perfect tense verb signifying a past completed action.

147 Peter also said, "30 The God of our ancestors raised up Jesus, whom you [Jewish religious leaders] had killed by hanging him on a tree. 31 God exalted him at his right hand as Leader and Savior that he might give repentance to Israel and forgiveness of sins. 32 And **we [apostles] are witnesses to these things, and so is the Holy Spirit** whom God has given to those who obey him" (Acts 5:30-32, emphasis mine).

148 See, for example, Acts 14:23 "And after they had appointed elders for them in each church, with prayer and fasting they entrusted them to the Lord in whom they had come to believe." Acts 15:41 "He [Paul] went through Syria and Cilicia, strengthening the churches." Acts 16:4-5 "As they [Paul and Timothy] went from town to town, they delivered to them for observance the decisions that had been reached by the apostles and elders who were in Jerusalem. So the churches were strengthened in the faith and increased in numbers daily." Also note the many cities and regions names in the Epistles.

149 *Gospelizers* are often trailblazers — "pioneering proclamation," "founding new missions," and "organizing new churches." G. B. Funderburk, *ZPEB*, s.v. "Evangelist," vol. 2, p. 419.

150 One can contrast these seven priorities with the following five insights of the early church curriculum provided by Maria Harris: *koinonia*, or community; *leiturgia*, coming together to pray and to represent Jesus in the breaking of bread; *didache*, the activity of teaching; *kerygma*, proclaiming the word of Jesus' resurrection; and *diakonia*, caring for those in need. Based on Acts 2. Maria Harris, *Fashion Me A People* (Louisville: Westminster John Knox Press, 1989), pp. 16, 17.

151 See *"leiturgeo,"* perform religious service, signifying public worship; cf. Acts 13:2, "worshiping."

152 John 1:18 "No one has ever seen God. It is God the only Son, who is close to the Father's heart, who has made him known."

[153] Cf. Ezra 7:10 "For Ezra had set his heart to study the law of the Lord, and to do it, and to teach the statutes and ordinances in Israel."

[154] "the church" (singular) Matthew 16:18; 18:17ff.; Acts 2:47; "churches" (plural) Acts 9:31; 15:41; 16:5; "each/every church," or "the church at..." (particular) Acts 8:1; 11:22; 13:1; 14:23; 1 Corinthians 1:2; 4:17. See also, "The Church," *Collected Writings of W. E. Vine* (Nashville: Thomas Nelson Publishers, 1996).

[155] "The church needs a structural conversion...'Could it possibly be...that God in his mercy does not allow the world to enter the church in its present form?'" Kritzinger, *Op. cit.,* chap. 2:2.3.2; and 4:7.3.

[156] A *gospelizing* Church is like an envoy in the army of the kingdom of God. The King, Christ Jesus, and His army are marching for battle toward enemy territory. *Gospelizers* are envoys sent ahead of their King's approaching armies. As they draw near to the enemy, these ambassadors are prepared to offer terms of peace to the enemy. There is still time to prevent the battle. Hostilities can cease, and benefits of the King's reign can end tyranny and provide abundant prosperity for all. The terms of peace require the enemy to "repent," and to submit to the rule of the coming King (i.e., become His subjects/disciples). However, there is also an ultimatum. If the enemy rejects the gracious proffer of peace given by the *Gospelizers,* judgment and destruction are certain. In wrath, the King is coming. Cf. *ISBE, Op. cit.,* vol. 3, p. 943. "As shoes for your feet put on whatever will make you **ready to proclaim the gospel of peace**" (Ephesians 6:15, emphasis mine).

[157] Deacon Roger Hicks, Greater Union Baptist Church, Chicago.

[158] *On Being Witnesses* gives four attitudes toward life: *"being," "identification," "ability to receive,"* and *"being a servant."* Kritzinger, *Op. cit.,* 2:3.4.

[159] A creative program is suggested in *On Being Witnesses.* The **Seven I's Program** consists of *Inspiration, Information, Interpretation, Involvement, Instruction, Investment, and Intercession.* The authors suggest churches use the program for a diagnosis and prognosis of missionary quality and dynamism. Kritzinger, *Op. cit.,* 2:2.3.2.5.

¹⁶⁰ For example, the Cooperative Missions Network of the African Diaspora (COMINAD; www.reconciliationnetwork.org /cominad), is a great networking resource for Blacks who desire to do mission work.

¹⁶¹ Kritzinger, *Op. cit.*, 2.5.

¹⁶² Larger may mean a sanctuary that holds 1,000, 1,500, 5,000, or whatever the number of people.

¹⁶³ Usually, the purpose or motivation for construction is a larger worship sanctuary, which for the most part contains (and restrains?) more Sunday-going members, who only come to church on a single day of the week. Many of those members fail to participate in other church activities, such as Bible study or prayer meeting, not to mention outreach.

¹⁶⁴ Also, relinquishing some "legal" fiduciary responsibilities could be advised. This is the spirit of the move made by the apostles, according to Acts 6:1-7. More than maintaining legal management of the Church, the apostles operated from a base of spiritual and moral leadership, service and appeal.

¹⁶⁵ Some very large congregations are doing great and praiseworthy mission works for Christ. However, solely a large church-house and membership roll do not produce spiritual maturity, Christ-centered disciples, effective Gospelizers, or necessarily please God. Genuine Church growth springs from spiritual factors at work in the lives of believers and the center of church fellowship and operations. Successful mission-minded mega-churches have captured the spiritual essence of ministry, and as a result, are growing. Yet, for the cause of Christ and His kingdom, they could exponentially grow more by decentralizing and multiplying their successes.

¹⁶⁶ New churches should be **"Christonomous,"** and exist in unity in an interdependent, mutual, and reciprocal relationship with the planting church and sister churches. Both paternalism and autonomy are ruled out. Kritzinger, *Op. cit.*,1.3.5.1.

¹⁶⁷ *The Holy Bible: The Jubilee Legacy Bible* (Nashville: Townsend Press, 1999), p. 23; *Encyclopedia of Black America*, "Fisk Jubilee Singers" (New York: De Capo Press, Inc., 1981), p. 386.

¹⁶⁸ Valerie Gladstone, "Stepping and Stomping in an Old-Time Gospel Mood," *New York Times*, June 2, 2002, Sec. "Dance," p. 24.

Scripture Index

Scripture Index

Scripture Index

Subject Index

Subject Index

E

Early Church and believers, ix, 4, 5, 74, 75, 85, 106, 112, 130, 145, 204

Eternal, 2, 49

Ethiopian Official, 69, 93, 95, 132, 195

Euangelistes, vii, ix, 3, 42, 170, 171, 181, 190, 192, 196, 219

Euangelizo, vii, ix, xii, 3, 41, 42, 52-54, 57, 84-86, 90, 94, 95, 97-99, 170, 175, 180, 181, 183, 184, 186, 190-192, 196, 207

    in *1 Corinthians 9*, 97, 150, 171, 181, 194

    definition, 52, 53

    in *Galatians 1*, 35, 37, 43, 85, 94, 96-98, 171, 181, 182, 184, 191, 194

    intensive use, 85, 94, 99

    translations of, 3

Evangelist(s), 3, 4, 42, 47, 69, 73, 95, 171, 181-183, 186, 190, 192, 204

F

Fears, 29, 161

"feet of Gospelizers," i, iv, 45, 58, 100, 169

Fellowship, 6, 9, 23, 30, 57, 95, 106, 112-114, 128, 129, 133, 140, 141, 144, 149, 154, 194, 204, 207, 210

Fellowship and Pray, 138

Fisk Jubilee Singers, 167, 210

G

Galatian, church, 95

God-sent messengers, vii, 4, 19, 40, 50

Good News/words, vii, viii, xii, 1-4, 6, 7, 17, 19, 21, 40, 42-47, 49, 50, 52, 53, 54, 76, 82, 100, 114, 118-120, 126, 127, 129, 155, 160, 175, 181, 192, 194

Gospel

    a trust, 107

    blessings, 17

    commission, preservation, transmission, 106-108

    content of Christian message, 42, 43

    effectual in redemption, 34, 36, 47, 54, 55, 57

    grace, truth, and power, 17, 19, 32-35, 41, 76

    Jesus, Subject and Author of, 44

    Luke's, 86

    revealed truth, revelation, 43, 50, 96, 99

    salvation, 31

    "the truth of the Gospel," 95, 97

    tradition, 44

    unique/authentic, 37, 96

Gospel in Gospelizers, 3, 43, 98-99

Gospel-centered ministries, 6, 30, 127, 128, 156

Gospelizer

    immediate significance, 43

    popularizing, 41

    recovered paradigm, 1, 39, 41

Gospelizer Jesus, ix, 62

Gospelizer models

    anonymous women, 4, 51, 88

    Antioch church, 130

    Apostle Paul, 72

    Apostle Peter, 73

    emerge amidst terror, ix. 74

    God, 56

    Jesus Christ, 4, 116

    John the Baptist, 66

    other Biblical characters, 39

    Paul and Barnabas, 70

    the persecuted church, 68

    Philip, Peter and John, 68

    "the Twelve" apostles, 67

    Timothy, 73

Gospelizers

    A Model Emerges Amidst Terror, ix, 74

    aims, 19, 41

Subject Index

Subject Index

69, 87-89, 92, 102, 116, 118,
131, 170, 184, 186, 195, 209
the Messiah, 92
the movement, 104
no substitute for, 37
opposes materialism, 89, 92,
98, 119
peace, 94
Peter, 93
Peter and John, 92
Philip, 92, 93
power and authority, 53
power over demons, 52, 54,
56, 64, 66, 87, 89, 116, 118, 163
protecting, 98
resistance to, 90
Samaria, 92
Savior's birth, 86, 94
Spirit, Holy Spirit, iv, 11, 12,
31, 33, 36, 44, 51, 53, 63, 68,
69, 72, 76, 86, 87, 90, 92-95,
104, 105, 109, 117, 120, 130-
135, 140, 142, 145, 146, 148,
161, 162, 168, 171, 172, 176,
182, 187, 188, 190, 191, 193,
196, 203, 205, 207, 208
stepping and praise-dancing, 168
substantive, 37, 59, 111
theology of, ix, xii, 5, 39, 84, 100
the *verb*, 3
urgency, 2, 9, 16, 20, 31, 32, 74
women supported mission, 88,
157
worthy ambition, 37
yielding rights, 97
Gospelizing IS, 58
Gospelizing theology, 84
Gracious works, viii, 4, 6, 19, 30, 40,
46, 50, 54, 57-59, 119, 120, 127,
128, 139, 155, 193, 194
Great Commission, 105
Great workings, viii, 4, 30, 33, 46,
50, 54, 55, 59, 68, 76, 92, 118, 120,
122, 125, 139, 194-196, 203

H

Harvest-fields, viii, ix, 19, 21, 30, 40,
58, 60, 65, 102, 103, 115, 116,
118-120, 122, 125, 127, 129, 134,
136, 142, 161, 167, 168
Healing, 53, 55, 57, 69, 76, 78, 87-90,
123-126, 139, 145, 166, 196
holistic, 123, 125
Heralding/*Kerusso*, 52, 54, 82, 131,
139, 190
Holistic
healing of Jesus, 124
holistic gospelizing, 120

I

iaomai, 123
Identity and paradigm, ix, 1, 3, 39
Identity, mission, and witness, 51
Impartation, 16, 30, 43, 53, 55, 56,
60, 92, 111, 118, 124, 193, 203
Impetus and imperative, ix, 1, 8
Inclusion in Christ's community, 112
Investing in Gospelizers, 151

J

Jesus
gospelizing mission of, 51
making disciples FOR, 110
Servant, 148
Jesus gospelizing
authenticated Himself, 87
for John the Baptist, 63
Jubilee to the poor, 62
shepherdless crowds, 65
with authority in the Temple, 65
with the "Twelve" and many
women, 64
Jesus gospelizing the poor, authenticated His mission, 88
Jesus' mission
fulfilling, 86
to gospelize, 87
Joyful Gospelizers
angels of heaven, 163

Subject Index

Subject Index

Bibliography and Resources

In addition to citations appearing in the Notes, the reader can refer to these and certain web sites for bibliographic materials and resources related to missions work.

Biblical Word Study and Exposition

Anchor Bible Dictionary. New York: Doubleday, 1992.

Arndt, William F., F. Wilbur Gringrich, and F. William Danker. *A Greek-English Lexicon of the New Testament and Other Early Christian Literature, revised and edited by Frederick William Danker.* 3rd ed. Chicago: University of Chicago Press, 1957, 2000.

Friedrich, B. *"Euangelizomai, Euangelion, Proeuangelizomai, Euangelistes"* in *Theological Dictionary of the New Testament,* Gerhard Kittle and Gerhard Friedrich, eds. Grand Rapids: Eerdmans Publishing, 1964, p. 719ff.

International Standard Bible Encyclopedia. Grand Rapids: Eerdmans Publishing, 1988.

Louw, Johannes P. and Eugene A. Nida. *Greek-English Lexicon of the New Testament: Based on Semantic Domains.* Electronic Edition, Logos Library System. New York: United Bible Societies, 1989.

Robertson, Archibald Thomas. *Word Pictures in the New Testament.* Nashville: Sunday School Board of the Southern Baptist Convention, 1933. Electronic Edition, Logos Library System. Nashville: Broadman Press, 1998.

Strong, James. *New Strong's Dictionary of Hebrew and Greek Words.* Electronic Edition, Logos Library System. Nashville: Thomas Nelson Publishers, 1997.

Vine, W. E. *The Collected Writings of W. E. Vine.* Electronic Edition, Logos Library System. Nashville: Thomas Nelson Publishers, 1997.

_____, Merrill F. Unger, and William White, Jr. *Vine's Complete Expository Dictionary of Old and New Testament Words*. Electronic Edition, Logos Library System. Nashville: Thomas Nelson Publishers, 1997.

Zodhiates, Spiros. *The Complete Word Study Dictionary, New Testament*. Electronic Edition, Logos Library System. Chattanooga: AMG, 2000.

Zondervan Pictorial Encyclopedia of the Bible. Grand Rapids: Zondervan, 1975.

Contemporary Issues

Barret, David and Todd Johnson. "The Scandal of World A" in *World Evangelism Center: Pointing the Way to the Least Evangelized*. Pasadena: William Carey Library, 2001 (www.gem-werc.org/scandal/htm).

Copher, Charles B. *Black Biblical Studies, An Anthology of Charles B. Copher: Biblical and Theological Issues on the Black Presence in the Bible*. Chicago: Black Light Fellowship, 1993.

The Holy Bible: The African American Jubilee Edition. New York: The American Bible Society, 1999.

The Holy Bible: Jubilee Legacy Bible. Nashville: Townsend Press, 1999.

Hummel, Charles E. *Tyranny of the Urgent*. Downers Grove: InterVarsity Press, 1994.

Kritzinger, J. J., P. G. J. Meiring, and W. A. Saayman. *On Being Witnesses*. South Africa: Orion Publishers, Halfway House, 1994.

McCray, Walter Arthur. *The Black Presence in the Bible: Discovering the Black and African Identity of Biblical Persons and Nations*. Chicago: Black Light Fellowship, 1990.

_____. *The Black Presence in the Bible and the Table of Nations (Genesis 10:1-32), with Emphasis on the Hamitic and Genealogical Line from a Black Perspective*. Chicago: Black Light Fellowship, 1990.

Simmons, Martha and Frank Thomas, eds. *9.11.01: African American Leaders Respond to an American Tragedy.* Valley Forge: Judson Press, 2002.

Christian Organizational Resources

Black Light Fellowship (BLF/USA)
P. O. Box 5369
Chicago, IL 60680-4311
(773) 826-7790
www.blacklightfellowship.com

Black Light Fellowship of Ghana (BLF/GHANA)
c/o Rev. Dr. J. B. Saforo, Africa Director
Black Light Fellowship of Ghana
P. O. Box 1357
BRAKWA International School
Greater Union Baptist Churches of Ghana
Mamprobi-Accra
Ghana, West Africa

Cooperative Missions Network of the African Diaspora (COMINAD)
Reconciliation Ministries Network, Inc.
Contact: Brian Johnson
www.cominad.org
Has extensive bibliographic and networking sources; e.g., *Bibliography for African American Global Missions* (2002), Brian Johnson, compiler, and *Blacks in Missions – Books, Periodicals* (2002), Vaughn Walston, compiler; also see COMINAD's "Missions List" and list of "Global Missions."

National Black Evangelical Association (NBEA)
P. O. Box 4311
Chicago, IL 60680-4311
(312) 733-1516
Contact: Ruth Bentley, Ph.D., Director of Administration
nbeachicago@aol.com
Coalition on HIV/AIDS and other resources.

U.S. Center for World Mission (USCWM) See: **African American Center for World Mission (AACWM)**
www.uscwm.org
Contact: Rev. Ivor Duberry, Director

World Evangelization Research Center (WERC)
www.gem-werc.org
See especially the report *Pointing the Way to the Least Evangelized* (www.gem-werc.org/scandal/scandal.htm).

World Relief (WR)
www.worldrelief.org/what_we_do/aids_ministries

Gospelizers! Terrorized and Intensified
Rev. Dr. Walter Arthur McCray

Copies may be purchased at your local bookstore, via the internet, or mail order from the publisher.

BLACK LIGHT FELLOWSHIP
P.O. Box 5369 • Chicago, IL 60680
(773) 826-7790 *FAX –* (773) 826-7792
www.gospelizers.com

Name _____

Address _____

_____

City _____ST_____ZIP_____

Phones (D) (_____) _____

(E) (_____) _____

Email: _____

Please send me: **Gospelizers! Terrorized and Intensified**
by **Rev. Dr. Walter Arthur McCray**

No. of copies _____ x $**9.95** = $_____

Shipping: $5.00/1 copy + .50 each addl. = $_____

TOTAL ENCLOSED (Check/MO): $_____

Visa/Master/Disc #_____

Expiration Date_____

Mail to, or   **BLACK LIGHT FELLOWSHIP**
Credit Card   P.O. Box 5369 • Chicago, IL 60680
FAX: *FAX –* (773) 826-7792

Convenient ordering coupon

Gospelizers!
Terrorized and Intensified

by **Rev. Dr. Walter Arthur McCray**

may be purchased

- *at your local bookstore*

- *via the internet*

- *from the publisher*

 BLACK LIGHT FELLOWSHIP
P.O. Box 5369
Chicago, IL 60680

Phone – **(773) 826-7790**   *FAX –* **(773) 826-7792**

www.gospelizers.com